A2 in a Week

General Studies

GW00546867

Where to find the information you need

SUCCESS OR YOUR MONEY BACK

Letts' market leading series A2 in a Week gives you everything you need for exam success. We're so confident that they're the best revision books you can buy that if you don't make the grade we will give you your money back!

HERE'S HOW IT WORKS

Register the Letts A2 in a Week guide you buy by writing to us within 28 days of purchase with the following information:

- Name
- Address
- Postcode
- Subject of A2 in a Week book bought

Please include your till receipt

To make a **claim**, compare your results to the grades below. If any of your grades qualify for a refund, make a claim by writing to us within 28 days of getting your results, enclosing a copy of your original exam slip. If you do not register, you won't be able to make a claim after you receive your results.

CLAIM IF...

You are an A2 (A Level) student and do not get grade E or above. You are a Scottish Higher level student and do not get a grade C or above.

This offer is not open to Scottish students taking SCE Higher Grade, or Intermediate qualifications.

Letts Educational
Chiswick Centre
414 Chiswick High Road
London W4 5TF

Tel: 020 8996 3333
Fax: 020 8742 8390
e-mail: mail@lettsed.co.uk
website: www.letts-education.com

First published 2001

Text © Francis Beswick 2001
Design and illustration © Letts Educational Ltd 2001

British Library Cataloguing in Publication Data
A CIP record for this book is available from the British Library.

ISBN 1 85805 927 5

Prepared by *specialist* publishing services, Milton Keynes

Printed in Italy

Letts Educational Limited is a division of Granada Learning Limited, part of the Granada Media Group

Registration and claim address:

Letts Success or Your Money Back Offer, Letts Educational, Chiswick Centre, 414 Chiswick High Road, London W4 5TF

TERMS AND CONDITIONS

1. Applies to the Letts A2 in a Week series only
2. Registration of purchases must be received by Letts Educational within 28 days of the purchase date
3. Registration must be accompanied by a valid till receipt
4. All money back claims must be received by Letts Educational within 28 days of receiving exam results
5. All claims must be accompanied by a letter stating the claim and a copy of the relevant exam results slip
6. Claims will be invalid if they do not match with the original registered subjects
7. Letts Educational reserves the right to seek confirmation of the level of entry of the claimant
8. Responsibility cannot be accepted for lost, delayed or damaged applications, or applications received outside of the stated registration/claim timescales
9. Proof of posting will not be accepted as proof of delivery
10. Offer only available to A2 students studying within the UK
11. SUCCESS OR YOUR MONEY BACK is promoted by Letts Educational, Chiswick Centre, 414 Chiswick High Road, London W4 5TF
12. Registration indicates a complete acceptance of these rules
13. Illegible entries will be disqualified
14. In all matters, the decision of Letts Educational will be final and no correspondence will be entered into

Introduction

This book follows on from AS in a Week General Studies. Its focus is slightly different from AS in a Week, which emphasised skills. Here the aim is to examine broad outlines of the areas that are covered by the course.

The areas covered are as follows:

A: Culture Section

- Society and Culture: the ways in which society and culture interact.

- Religious Cultures: the influence of religion upon cultures.

- Belief and Art: how philosophical and religious beliefs are expressed in art.

- The Power of the Media: the way in which the media exerts influence in society and culture.

B: Society and Politics Section

- Ideology and Values: a look at beliefs about society and politics.

- Political Processes: how societies are run.

- Explanation and Behaviour: the ways in which behaviour can be explained.

- Ethical Issues: resolving ethical problems.

C: Science Section

- Nature of Reality: what reality is made of.

- Moral Responsibility: the responsibilities that come with scientific knowledge.

- Science and Culture: how science and technology influence cultures.

D: Synoptic Section

- The synoptic section shows how to link up ideas from a range of areas.

Society and Culture

10 minutes

Test your knowledge

1 Give a definition of society.

2 Define culture.

3 What is a pluralist society?

4 What is multicultural education?

5 Most cultures in Britain share a common _____ heritage.

6 If we want to evaluate a culture, or be critical of it, we must make a _____ judgment.

7 There has recently been a revival of interest in minority languages, such as Manx or Cornish. Why is this so?

Answers

1 a body of people who share common institutions 2 a shared set of beliefs, values and rules 3 a society that tolerates many cultures 4 educating children to live in a multicultural society 5 European 6 value 7 to express national identities

✔ **If you got them all right, skip to page 11**

Society and Culture

Improve your knowledge

1 Society

Society is a broad term covering groups of people who share a common life in some way. It can denote human relationships on a national scale, for example British society with all its shared public institutions and traditions. It can also refer to smaller-scale societies, such as religious or minority ethnic groups, which may possess their own rules and institutions as far as their internal affairs are concerned. The term society can also refer to voluntary institutions that operate for a purpose shared by their members, such as the Royal Society for the Prevention of Cruelty to Animals, a group of people who share a common concern for animals and who co-operate to express this concern.

'Society' can refer to a number of groupings.

It is essential that any kind of society possesses some rules and institutions in common, otherwise it is just a collection of individuals living near to each other. Society of any kind requires some kind of social contract, an agreement to live under certain rules. This may not be explicitly signed – we may implicitly consent to it by living in a society and enjoying its benefits.

2 Culture

A culture is a set of beliefs and values and the rules, institutions and customs that derive from them. One example of a country that is culturally nearly homogeneous (where everyone shares the same culture) is Saudi Arabia. There the religion is Islam, which specifies the beliefs and values that are required for citizenship of that country, and which is the basis of its laws. There is an agreed authority structure, running from the king down through various public authorities and tribal elders, and there are customs such as the public dress code for women and the ban on alcohol that are nationally accepted. Although some people flout these laws, as is the case with all laws, few are currently prepared to argue for their being changed. All these elements constitute Saudi culture. This is an example of a culture that is linked with a specific country. Yet the link between country and culture can be less precise than this. We might talk of northwest European cultures, those found in a broad area of northwest

Our culture is what we believe and how we put it into practice.

5

Society and Culture

Europe. We might talk of green culture – the beliefs, values, institutions and customs of the green movement. Thus culture is a broad term covering a variety of different situations.

Culture is expressed in various cultural artefacts and artistic practices. These include the visual arts, music, forms of dancing and drama that arise within a culture and which may be characteristic of it.

3 Pluralist societies

You can see from the above example that there are variations in the relationship between society and culture. The United Kingdom is a pluralist society, one of which you can be a member without subscribing to any system of beliefs or values. You can be a Christian, Muslim, atheist, socialist, etc., and still be a UK citizen. The legal institutions of the UK reflect this situation, for its laws are intended to enable people to live peacefully according to their conscience. A multicultural society is one in which a significant number of different cultures live side by side. The UK is both pluralist and multicultural, as it has a large number of cultures, all of which live on an equal basis. But a society can be pluralist without being multicultural. The Irish Republic was always pluralist in that it respected rights of freedom of conscience, but until recently, most of the country consisted of Irish Catholics who shared the dominant culture, so it was not a multicultural society.

A society might contain several cultures.

Anyone discussing culture and society will soon run into the problem that tensions arise between different cultures within a multicultural society or one that has any cultural minorities, however small.

- The key issue is the tension that occurs between what behaviour minorities accept and majorities allow. In the United Kingdom there is a tension between Rastafarians, whose religion enjoins that they smoke marijuana, and the law, which outlaws its use. The marriage customs of some Asian cultures in the UK involve arranged marriages, and some girls have been forced to marry against their will. This runs contrary to British values regarding human rights.

- Arising from the minority–majority tension is an important ethical issue: how far can respect for cultural freedoms go? Let us take, for example, the practice of female circumcision performed by some immigrant communities, in which girls are sexually mutilated by the removal of sexually sensitive tissue. This is not allowed in the UK, but is the norm in some African Muslim societies. The tension is whether a pluralistic society that respects religious freedom should allow such practices to be performed on infants, as this will constrain the infants' choices in the future. Should respect for an infant's future personal freedom outweigh respect for cultural freedoms for the infant's community? British law decides in favour of future personal freedom and bans this practice.

- We still have to decide the boundary between the rights of minority cultures and the rights of the state. If a cultural majority imposes its way of life on minorities, we soon have an intolerant society; yet sometimes what a minority culture is doing may be offensive to the majority. The issue is whether or not what a culture is doing impedes freedom in the future. Female circumcision impedes choice, but merely teaching minority beliefs does not. The former is banned, while the latter is not.

 4 Culture and education

Education and culture are intertwined, as education involves the sharing of culture between the educator and those to be educated. Education necessarily involves transmitting ideas, stories, skills, attitudes, etc., which are thought to be valuable, and thus we can never disentangle education from values. Societies transmit through the education system what their culture deems to be valuable. In societies politically dominated by one culture, only that culture is transmitted in schools. Other cultures are mentioned, but in a disparaging way so as to foster the dominant culture. Pluralist societies attempt to distance education from the control of the dominant culture, allowing other cultures a say in the education system. Distancing education from the control of the dominant culture is essential to the proper functioning of liberal democracies, which are democracies that allow individuals to choose to live a variety of lifestyles and by whatever philosophy or religion they choose. Allowing other cultures representation in the education system is a means of allowing them to flourish, which would not happen were one culture to control education.

Without transmission through education, cultures die.

This leads us to consider important issues regarding how such representation can be made.

- The educational curriculum may allow for multicultural teaching, in which students study a variety of cultures.

- Teaching of controversial issues is generally impartial so as not to foster the beliefs of the government of the day.

- Cultural minorities may be allowed to have their own schools. These may be religious minorities, but independent education allows freedom for unorthodox educational philosophies to flourish. Sunday schools for Christians, mosque schools for Muslims and Hebrew schools for Jewish children express the way in which cultural pluralism is reflected in the education system.

- Parents may have a right to withdraw children from some lessons, such as religious and sex education.

Yet there is a danger of such independent/religious schools creating cultural ghettoes in which children only have exposure to their own culture. To avoid this problem, cultural freedoms must be matched by corresponding obligations to broaden the students' cultural horizons.

5 The European dimension

As the world becomes more complex, it becomes harder to be in just one society and one cultural group. A person living in Manchester, for example, will be part of English society, but also part of a wider British society, which itself is part of European society. These three levels of society have specific and interacting political identities, and you can belong to all three societies simultaneously. There is a broader European dimension to culture as well. British culture is not something unique and distinct from the culture of the European mainland. Britain has taken ideas from the Continent since well before Roman times, and the Continent has also taken ideas from Britain. The French intellectuals of the Enlightenment, an eighteenth-century movement that proclaimed the value of reason, were strongly influenced by John Locke and other seventeenth-century English thinkers. Christianity was brought to

British cultures are part of European culture.

Britain from the Continent, and its division into Catholic and Protestant is of European origin.

The United Kingdom shares institutions in common with Europe. The European Union deals with matters that cannot in the modern world easily be handled at national level. The European Court of Human Rights (not an EU institution) was developed by British lawyers after World War II, and is thus not a foreign court overruling us, but one in which the United Kingdom has an equal influence established by treaty.

6 Can we evaluate cultures?

Evaluating anything involves making a value judgment, which measures it against a standard. To evaluate a culture or cultural artefact or tradition is to measure it against a standard often set by another culture. This is somewhat problematic, as doing so assumes that one culture is the benchmark of value for others. This may be true, but it can also reflect cultural arrogance.

Values influence judgments.

The question, then, is whether some cultures are higher than others, a question that can only be construed as asking whether some are more valuable than others. At some extremes we must say that they are: the culture and society of Nazi Germany was inferior on moral criteria to that of its neighbours, although this does not imply perfection among the neighbours. But can we compare the arts of different cultures? Is it possible to say that classical ballet is a higher art form than Irish dancing? Does society's elevation of one over the other reflect a difference in the level of skill involved, or merely the preferences of the dominant class or culture? We can see that values do influence judgments.

7 Language and culture

Contradictory forces are at work: minority languages are suffering from the economic dominance of major ones, especially those used on television; but strong cultural movements fight to keep them alive. Cornish and Manx have been revived by enthusiasts. The reason for their enthusiasm is that language and cultural identity are linked. For the Cornish to assert their identity as a Celtic nation in England, but not an Anglo-Saxon one, they need to have a

Language contains a culture's beliefs and values.

language and a body of literature written in it. This does not mean that there is any hope or threat that it will replace English, but it will provide a means by which a culture can express itself. Such minority languages and cultures, though often only kept alive by small numbers of enthusiasts, perform the vital function of counteracting the global dominance of Atlantic culture. This is dominated by mainstream American culture as transmitted by television, which is in danger of eradicating local cultures by its sheer economic strength. Minority languages provide alternative ways of expressing meaning and sometimes saying things in ways that other languages cannot.

Reflections

We can see that culture and society interact in complex, and sometimes problematic, ways. There is the serious ethical issue of where the line can be drawn between respecting minority cultures and preventing intolerable behaviour that denies human rights. In an examination, you could use the examples of female circumcision and forced marriages. There is also the problem of how to free aesthetic judgments from unconscious social influences regarding what is high status and what is not. Finally, there is the issue of the status of ethnic minority languages in a world where a dominant culture is being fostered by the mass media. You should ask yourself what benefits ethnic minorities can gain from preserving their own language and how the preservation of their own cultures can sustain cultural variety in the world.

Society and Culture

Use your knowledge

Read the following passage and answer the questions.

The 'coca-cola culture' is being imposed on the world by American economic dominance. Everywhere western-style consumer goods flood markets and edge out local cultural products, which are rapidly declining to the status of curios sold to tourists by vendors who go home to a western lifestyle, enjoying western goods and watching western television programmes. How many of the artists who create them are simply copying the art of a culture in which they no longer believe? If this trend continues, we will soon have a bland, worldwide western culture in which all cultural variety is eradicated. Yet all is not lost. A counter-trend is emerging in which enthusiasts foster local cultures and minority languages. The revival of Manx, for instance, allows for poetry, literature and song to be created in that tongue. Each language has its own 'music' – its rhythms and rhymes that enable it to flow. Losing ethnic minority languages denies humanity the unique poetry and song that arises from them. It is only through the vigorous promotion of local and minority cultures that we can prevent a bland, worldwide monoculture from emerging.

1 Why do you think American culture is termed 'coca-cola culture'?

2 What does the author mean by speaking of 'the music of a language'?

3 Why is the author critical of the artists who make some of the goods sold to tourists? Is this a fair criticism?

4 Assess the advantages and disadvantages of preserving minority languages. (Your answer should be a paragraph or so in length.)

10 minutes

Test your knowledge

1 Religions have a set of beliefs and values that form part of their _____ _____.

2 Their beliefs and values are expressed in _____.

3 All religions have their own _____ laws.

4 Religious cultures need a system of _____ so that their beliefs and values can be transmitted through generations.

5 Religious cultures always have sacred _____.

Answers

1 world view 2 customs 3 moral 4 education 5 spaces

✔ **If you got them all right, skip to page 18**

Religious Cultures

35 minutes

Improve your knowledge

1 Every one of us has a world view, which is a general understanding of what the world is like. It includes the answers to the following questions:

Key points from AS in a Week

Religion and Theology
pages 12–13

- What kinds of beings are there in the world (e.g. God, angels, matter, mind, etc.)?
- How do things happen in the world (e.g. through physical causes, magic, activities of divine beings, etc.)?
- What is human nature? Are we just matter, or do we have a spiritual soul?
- What can humans know about this world and the other, if there is one?
- What is death, and what happens beyond it?

Religions have a religious world view.

Religions have their own world views, which differ from nonreligious world views. For example, a Humanist (a nonreligious person who believes in respect for persons) will disbelieve in God and believe that ethical rules are about the relationships between humans and each other (along with some animals). He or she will leave God out of the picture and will regard death as the end beyond which there is nothing. On the other hand, for religious believers, God is real. God has to be the source of all ethical rules and must be included in all moral decision-making. Most religious people believe that after death their actions will be in some way rewarded or punished. It should be clear then that religious and nonreligious people will live different lifestyles. We can say therefore that religious cultures differ from nonreligious cultures in the following ways:

- Things that matter to one will not matter to the other.
- They will have different values.
- They will have different purposes in life.
- They will differ in their perception of events in society and nature.
- Their impact on society and nature will reflect their values.

You should bear these differences in mind when responding to questions that make reference to a religious culture, as this will help improve your understanding.

Religious Cultures

2 Religious world views give rise to cultural practices that express the beliefs and values contained in them, and sometimes these can look very strange to people who do not understand them. For example, when some people see a group of Muslims praying by kneeling on mats and bowing while they face Mecca, they might think that such practices are strange. But people realise that they make perfect sense when they understand the thinking behind them. Muslims face Mecca because facing their sacred city reminds them that they all belong to one community and not to a host of different ones. Similarly, their bowing is a way of saluting God, whom they regard as their king; they use mats so that they can be clean for prayer, again a sign of respect for God. Similarly, certain people find the Hindu idea of meditating while concentrating on the sound 'om' to be a strange practice, but it makes sense, as 'om' is the sacred syllable of the Hindu faith, and concentrating on it is used as a means of attaining the depths of meditation to which the Hindu faith aspires. These points should alert you to the fact that customs that seem meaningless to one person are deeply meaningful to others, and that they only seem strange to those who do not understand them.

Cultural practices arise out of world views.

Religious cultures generally have festivals, which

* express their beliefs and values

* act as social occasions when community bonding can be strengthened

* enable people to enjoy their religion, which is especially important after a period of fasting (for example, the Easter festival, when Christians celebrate Jesus' resurrection from the dead, follows the gloomy days of Lent and Holy Week, when Jesus' passion is recalled).

Religious cultures have their own styles of art. Muslim culture, for example, has few pictures but much use of patterns, as Muslims disapprove of the representation of the human form and will never visually represent God. Hinduism, on the other hand, has a long tradition of visual art and happily represents its deities in visual form. Religions also develop their own religious music.

Religious Cultures

3 Religious cultures generally have their own moral codes. This is a controversial area, as Humanists argue that morality should be autonomous of religion, meaning that it does not require a religious basis. While it is correct that you can be moral without being religious, it is also the case that religious world views give rise to moral and ethical beliefs that differ from nonreligious moral codes. These moral rules go beyond the rules which form the basic requirement for social living that nonreligious ethical systems prescribe.

Religions express themselves in moral codes.

For example, religions can be stricter on issues of sexual morality than nonreligious ethics are. Christians are generally strict on sex outside marriage, and the Muslim dress code for women, which insists on public modesty, is the strictest in the world. The reasons for this strictness are not always easy to identify, but it probably arises out of the religious beliefs that:

- Sex and family life go together in God's design for life.

- The breakdown of relationships causes much heartbreak, so to avoid this pain we should restrict ourselves to sex in enduring marriages.

- Uncontrolled sex leads to emotional and social problems.

- Sex ought to be constrained in order to facilitate spiritual growth.

These rules are generally less relevant for nonreligious ethics, which do not prescribe that we live according to God's plan, and do not have the same ideas on spiritual growth as believers do.

Religions have rules about worship that cannot be present in nonreligious ethical systems. These rules draw their value from the religion's belief that there is a deity who is to be taken seriously and given appropriate respect.

If in an examination (or in life) you encounter a reference to moral rules or practices that seems strange or meaningless to you, be aware that these rules belong to moral systems that arise from views of human nature and the ultimate destiny of humans that you might not share or understand. It is important not to prejudge them but to give them a sympathetic hearing.

Religious Cultures

4 Religious cultures need a method of transmitting their beliefs and values to later generations, or else they will die out.

Religions only survive by transmitting themselves through the generations.

- Beliefs and values are transmitted.
- This enables members of a religion to live out their beliefs and values, as practice is essential if people are to develop within their religious faith.
- Sometimes cultural transmission involves extra forms of schooling to supplement state schooling, which transmits the dominant culture.
- In the United Kingdom, there are denominational schools belonging to Christians (mainly Roman Catholics), Jews and Muslims. These schools are partly state-run.
- Independent schools often have a religious character, as they are established by faith communities so that they can run on their lines and teach their values.

Schooling in addition to mainstream education is common. Christians have Sunday school; many Jews attend Hebrew school, where they learn Hebrew and the scriptures; Muslims have mosque school, which they attend in the evenings and where they learn the Koran.

Cultural transmission might also occur in other ways:

- Through religious services, which believers attend on certain days. Christians attend church on Sundays, where they hear the minister preach about their faith. Muslims and Jews attend mosque and synagogue respectively for the same purposes.
- Through religious broadcasting and publishing. Religious publishers of books and newspapers are common in all faiths.

This transmission takes place through the means of authorised ministers who have acquired some expertise in a faith. Jews have *rabbis* deeply versed in Jewish scholarship; Hindus have *pandits* who are wise in Hindu learning; Christians have various kinds of ministers; Muslims have *imams* learned in the Koran. These ministers attend various kinds of training courses to obtain their status.

5 Religious cultures generally possess sacred spaces, places that have a religious function. These may be churches, mosques, temples, etc., where believers gather for the official services of their faith. There are also shrines, sites special to a god, goddess or saint, or places where an event of religious significance has occurred. The design of these places is determined by the teachings of the faith to which it belongs. Christian churches often have a spire, the tower that points heavenwards as a sign that Christians aim for heaven. Mosques have few if any seats, as they need to have space for the worshippers to bow down. However, sacred spaces need not be buildings. They can be clearings in a forest, caves, gardens or enclosures open to the sky, as Stonehenge was.

Religions need places that are holy to them.

The importance of these sacred spaces is that they create an area which a religious community can call its own, in which its people can congregate and in which the community can operate its own rituals. They enable worshippers to create environments whose art, architecture and character express their beliefs and values.

Shrines are a way of preserving the memory of a great event by preserving the sacred space associated with it, and giving it a solid, enduring architectural expression that can be the focus for public worship. For example, the shrine at Lourdes recalls the strange experiences of Bernadette Soubirous, a young woman who claimed to have seen a vision of Mary, the mother of Jesus. The site of her experiences has been enclosed and appropriately decorated and is now a popular destination for pilgrims, who participate in the cult that has grown up around the site.

Reflections

After reading this you should have gained some understanding of religious culture and seen how it has to express its world view in rituals, customs and moral codes, and how it must mark out some sacred spaces and times for its worshippers to express their beliefs and values. You should have understood that religious believers will make their mark on their social and natural environment.

15 minutes

Use your knowledge

Read the following passage and answer the questions.

The Monastic Haven

In northern Europe, a very similar pattern emerged. Big business bought up the original small land holdings and created vast estates, run as aggressively as any major agribusiness today. By the end of the 5th century AD, much of modern-day France, Belgium, southern Germany and England was a waste land of over-exploited soil and lost tree cover. It was into this destruction that Christianity brought healing of the land and of nature through the farming and gardening techniques developed especially by the Benedictine monastic order, founded in AD 515.

The rise of monastic Christianity was a reaction against Roman, urban Christianity. It led to the restoration of agriculture and horticulture, which created the farms, gardens and beauty of so much of northern Europe in the centuries after Rome and whose passing through the changes in agriculture today we so mourn. The rolling green hills and fields, orchards, streams full of fresh water, the village ponds, gardens, herbs and flowers for our use – all and more of this beauty we owe to the pioneering, loving and Godly work of the monks and nuns. They not only developed best practice in woodland management, drainage, soil enrichment, fertilisers, orchards, vineyards, pleasure gardens and herbal gardens, but they also wrote much of it down and helped preserve the wisdom of the classical writers on plants. Medicine – virtually all of it herbal – was a major factor of every monastery and required intimate knowledge of the properties of plants and flowers.

Christian architecture has long celebrated nature through its carvings, stained glass and misericords. For example, the Chapter House at Southwell Cathedral in Nottinghamshire, England, provides one of the most important visual records of common plants of the early Middle Ages. Carved on every corbel, arch and capital is a mass of plants and flowers, accurate in very detail.

The essence of the monastic garden is a Christian fusion between place and space, plants and symbolism, usefulness and beauty, all caught up in a vision of nature, humanity and God as being in a unity of purpose and intention.

(from *Sacred Gardens* by Martin Palmer and David Manning)

Religious Cultures

1 Explain the role of the monasteries in 'healing' the land after the Roman Empire fell.

2 'Christian architecture has long celebrated nature.'
   (a) What evidence does the author give for this claim?
   (b) Why do you think Christian architecture celebrates nature?

3 The author says that a Christian garden is 'a fusion between … usefulness and beauty'. What do you think he means by this statement?

Belief and Art

10 minutes

Test your knowledge

1 'Art has no connection with philosophical or religious beliefs.' True or false?

2 Which of the following ancient thinkers believed that art (poems, stories, etc.) was a very inferior activity?
(a) Plato
(b) Aristotle
(c) St Paul

3 'Art should _____ show you reality as it is.' Choose the correct option from the three below.
(a) always
(b) never
(c) sometimes

4 *Ars gratia artis* is a well-known phrase which means:
(a) Artists like art.
(b) Art for art's sake.
(c) Art should be free for everyone.

5 'Pornography corrupts those who view it.' Choose the correct answer from the selection below.
(a) always true
(b) never true
(c) maybe in some cases

Answers

1 false 2 (a) 3 (c) 4 (b) 5 (c)

 If you got them all right, skip to page 26

Belief and Art

Improve your knowledge

 Art is work made by human skill as opposed to what is found naturally, but often we restrict the term to the products of the creative arts: the visual arts, music, dance, theatre, craft, etc. Unlike objects that are merely useful, these speak to us in some way and address our emotional and spiritual needs. Of course, useful objects can also be works of art. Cooking can be an exquisite art form, but its usefulness is undeniable.

Art of any kind arises from the artist's mind, and so it will be affected by their beliefs and values. For example, take a look at this Celtic cross. This type of cross was produced by Irish monks in the first millennium AD. The cross is obviously a Christian symbol for Christ, but the ring around it represents the sun. The ancient Irish believed that the presence of God radiated through nature in and through the sun's light, so a sun symbol is linked to the cross. You will also see Bible scenes upon its stem, as visual aids to help the monks preach. The intricately intertwined beasts on the stem derive from ancient Celtic art, and they represent the beauty, complexity and wonder of nature as designed by God. You can see how these monks were heirs to Christian and ancient Celtic cultural influences and how, therefore, the two strands combined in their imaginations to produce the Celtic crosses. The blending of Christian and ancient Celtic symbols shows that God is known through nature and the Bible.

Any work of human hands can be called art if it expresses and communicates ideas and feelings.

The monks who produced these crosses had something important to say to their fellows, and they used art to do it. This is so with all great artists; they have a vision or a set of feelings that they want to put into a form that can be shared by others, and through which they want to influence, direct or shape others' lives for the better.

Belief and Art

2 People can have very different attitudes to art. The ancient Greek philosopher, Plato, had quite a low view of art, especially poetry, which he thought was the enemy of philosophy. For Plato, truth could only be found by reason and could be best expressed in reasoned language, so he thought that philosophy was the highest form of knowledge, followed closely by mathematics. In these two subjects there was no room for the techniques of art. Knowledge of the natural world was also lower than mathematics, and right at the bottom of the scale were the arts, which Plato thought gave a false view of the world. He believed that art was fiction, or at best a poor representation of reality which was worth less than the reality that it represented.

Few people have gone as far as Plato, as most people feel that art can say some things that philosophical language cannot say, and that it has a power to touch our hearts and minds in ways that reasoned discourse cannot. For example:

Art is a way of communicating what we deeply believe and feel.

- A story or a picture can have more impact on us than an explanation.
- We express our emotions in music, dance and poetry; music can affect our emotions very greatly.
- Art can sometimes express ideas that ordinary language cannot; religions use music and poetry to express the inexpressible, the God whom they worship.
- Art is a way of accessing aspects of reality beyond the reach of science.

Take the example of a Greek icon, one of the holy pictures found in Greek churches. To be allowed to paint an icon, a monk must have reached a certain standard of holiness, as judged by his abbot. Icons are therefore the expressions not just of ideas, but of the inner, spiritual lives of those who paint them. The inner life cannot be described in scientific, philosophical or mathematical terms, and so it must be expressed in symbolic form. Worshippers focus on these icons when they are praying, and they often reflect on them during their meditation because:

- The icons can help focus their thoughts on the spiritual aspects of life.
- They believe that the icons are a window on the higher reality that enables them to draw nearer to it.

Belief and Art

Art does not
always have to
copy reality.

 3 How far does art have to represent reality? Should art show us reality as it is, just as a photograph does? Although, when you look at a photograph, it is more than just a visual image, as the photographer often intends you to feel something – maybe to marvel at the beauty of what is seen or feel compassion for the people portrayed.

There are aspects of reality which we cannot portray in visual form. While we can certainly represent an object, a place or a person, how can visual imagery adequately represent meaning? The feelings of characters in a picture cannot be shown as they are, as feelings have no visible form. So to represent them, artists must use visual clues, such as the characters' gestures and facial expressions.

Often art uses visual symbolism to express the artist's ideas. In religious pictures you see characters with haloes, which are an artistic convention to signify that the character is a good one, a saint rather than a sinner. Art, therefore, need not always be a photograph of reality, as it can speak in visual symbols of realities that cannot be portrayed directly. Dance and theatre do not show reality as it is, but represent it in a symbolic form.

Some art forms cannot provide images of reality, as they are non-visual. Music, for example, has a peculiar relationship to the visible world. We may be stirred to compose music by the sight of beauty, for example an attractive person or something in nature. Holst was inspired to write music by his thoughts on the planets and the emotions that the grandeur of the heavens aroused. What music produces is not visual but evocative; it conveys the emotions that such visions produce, and can stir the imagination to create images that match the emotions.

Art sometimes represents reality as it might be or ought to be. Playwrights may try to depict situations that might possibly occur, so as to alert the audience to dangers in society. Artists of all kinds may also try to depict society as they believe it ought to be. Communist art, produced in the former Soviet Union, depicted the workers rising against their masters, and sometimes there were images of the post-revolutionary world when all would be equal and happy. These images were intended to foster communist commitment in the people.

Belief and Art

4 The widely known saying, 'art for art's sake' is an answer to the question of what art is for. The belief that underlies this statement is that art only needs to convey aesthetic values, the type of values which include beauty and good taste. Most people expect works of art to be beautiful, and they feel that artists should work for the creation of beauty. Yet when we examine art we do not find that people value them only for their beauty. A work of art might be quite the opposite of beautiful, but it is a work of art nonetheless. For example, some wartime photographers produced powerful images of the Nazi concentration camps. No one could say that what they showed was beautiful, as it was ugly and evil, but it served the vitally important purpose of showing reality for what it was. This kind of art may indeed be the product of high artistic skill, but its purpose is not to show beauty, but truth. In the field of modern art, some artists set out to shock the viewers in the hope of stirring them out of the complacency that the artist assumes they have. The artists want their audience to take a new perspective on life. So again we see that art is not just about beauty, as some artists intend to educate.

Art might also aim to heal minds or to create desirable moods. If you listen to Gregorian chants, the music used by medieval Christian monks, you will appreciate how it aims to calm the emotions and put the mind into a tranquil state. Many ordinary people listen to this music when they feel stressed. New Age music sometimes has a similar purpose, and New Age therapists often use calming music as part of their healing practice.

Art can have therapeutic purposes.

The arts speak to us about human life, and stimulate us to think about the important issues that beset us, such as love, death, and the purpose for which we live. This is why religions, in particular, generate much visual art and music, and why some of them have elaborate rituals that convey their teachings in dramatic and symbolic form.

Belief and Art

 Should art have a moral character? Can art only be judged on aesthetic values or should we judge a work of art on its moral content? Can a painting or piece of music be called a work of art if it conveys a morally dubious or discreditable message? Could a work, highly regarded in terms of the skill that has gone into it and the aesthetic values found within, be criticised if its moral message was seen to be wrong? For example, could a novel that extols the pleasures of sexual violence (against either men or women) be regarded as a work of art, even if it were beautifully written?

Art can speak about moral issues.

Other examples might be the propaganda films produced for Hitler, which glorified Nazism. Some of these films were excellent examples of the film-maker's art, as their design and camera work were of a high standard, but we might argue that their glorifying of Hitler and his false values of arrogance and glory through military force means that they were morally flawed. Could we enjoy these films as fine examples of the art of film-making, knowing that the philosophy that they transmitted was evil and led to so much suffering?

Most of us would think that such films and novels are not art, as they are morally repulsive, but the issue is not always this simple. D H Lawrence's novel, *Lady Chatterley's Lover*, was banned as pornography, even though it was beautifully written, as it contained 'four-letter' Anglo-Saxon words that were considered shocking at the time and some vivid sex scenes. However, lawyers successfully opposed the ban on the grounds that:

- its English was of a superb standard
- the author only used the 'offensive' words because he wanted to restore them to daily use as respectable English words
- he was arguing a reasonable case against conventional sexual ethics.

That this was not just a dirty book soon became clear, and the ban was lifted. Whether its author was right or wrong about sexual ethics is debatable, but he was certainly using the novel to discuss important issues about morality and language. Thus we account it a work of art, even if we do not agree with all the views contained in it. We might say that art can have a moral character, but we ought not to make simplistic judgments on artistic works.

Belief and Art

15 minutes

 **your knowledge**

Read the following passage and answer the questions.

Dear Sir

I must protest about the use of tax payers' money to purchase pieces of modern 'art'. I have just seen Damian Hirst's offering, a dead sheep floating in preservative, and a mass of bricks that I am told have been 'tastefully' arranged. This stuff is just not art; anyone with a little skill can do it. In earlier times people knew what art was for: it was about creating beautiful pictures. Great artists produced landscapes and seascapes that showed you what the beauties of the natural world were like; and there are inspiring pictures in our churches that lead you to contemplate spiritual affairs and our eternal destiny. 'Modern artists' are just a bunch of con men, selling rubbish and calling it art.

Yours faithfully,

Disgruntled of Anytown

1 Why does the writer place certain words in quotation marks?

2 According to this letter writer, what sorts of work count as good or great art?

3 What is the author's opinion of the importance of skill in art?

4 Comment on his statement that modern artists are just con men.

The Power of the Media

10 minutes

Test your knowledge

1 The media is a _____ through which we view our world.
Choose the correct word.
(a) lens
(b) tunnel
(c) angle

2 Those who run the media have to _____ which information to transmit.

3 The media can promote the _____ and _____ of those who own it.

4 It is possible for the media to _____ corruption by politicians and to _____ for political causes.

5 The media has a major role to play in creating _____.
Choose the correct word.
(a) lies
(b) hope
(c) culture

6 What do you think will be the effect of the development of the Internet and desktop publishing on the spread of information and ideas?

The Power of the Media

35 minutes

 your knowledge

1. The term 'the media' includes:

- newspapers and magazines
- television
- radio
- the Internet.

Key points from AS in a Week

Selection of Information pages 39–43

We can compare the media with a lens through which we look at the world because a lens in a telescope or eye glasses enables you to make barely visible objects more visible. The media brings to us information, ideas and experiences that we would not normally be able to obtain, and media organisations can collect a wide range of information that would take people engaged in other jobs too long to collect. This ability gives it enormous power.

The media brings the world to us.

Yet it is seldom a transparent window on the world. It can present a distorted or one-sided image, and it is possible for the media to tell untruths. This is especially so when control of the media is in the hands of a few powerful people and companies, and when these forces are in league with political parties, who use them to promote their views. Dictators seize control of the media soon after they take power, as they can use this control to stifle dissent. In Europe, the problem is not dictators having overall control, but the concentration of media power in a few hands, with the possibility that some views might be misrepresented or not represented at all. Most European states have rules as to how much media power a particular person or company can have, and these serve to ameliorate this problem. But the problem will not go away if those who control the media come from a narrow band in the political spectrum.

Smaller organisations usually have their own newspapers and magazines, but only a small minority of people buy them, so that those who own the national press are in a much more powerful position.

The Power of the Media

 All communication involves selection of information, so the media must select what is to be contained in their broadcasts and written materials. In principle, there is no wrong in this, but there can be some hidden dangers. The media might select to produce material which is relevant and informative, such as information about global warming, or it might produce material which merely aims to entertain and deals only in trivialities, such as that contained in many tabloid popular newspapers.

The media selects what information it will give us.

The selection of information made by any media outlet is determined by a number of factors:

- the specific philosophy or viewpoint that it is established to promote, if there is one
- the specific market which it serves; clearly it must meet the needs of its public if it is to stay in business.

Material might be omitted if it does not suit the purposes of those who report it. We often hear complaints that a major demonstration has gone unreported by the national media, or that an issue is not receiving the coverage that it deserves, at least in some people's eyes. These differences may be due to a genuine opinion that it is not newsworthy, or to the limited amount of time and space that a media outlet has available. However, it is also possible that material might be given no coverage because it does not suit the political or philosophical aims of those who control the media to publicise it.

When dealing with any item from the media, always be aware that the information has been selected, and that relevant information might have been left out to suit the media's purposes. This is especially true of television news, which has a short time to cover a wide range of issues.

 The media will usually promote the views and interests of those who control it. For example, religious and political organisations have their own newspapers, and sometimes television channels. Most people would say that this is acceptable as long as these organisations are honest and open about their aims and beliefs. However, there is a problem about the way in which newspapers reflect their owners' political views, especially if one organisation owns many news outlets, as happens with the giant News International, which owns newspapers and television interests around the world.

Media institutions promote the views of those who control them.

The Power of the Media

A media outlet might attempt to foster certain values. The *Daily Telegraph* openly fosters right-wing, conservative values, while the *Guardian* sometimes takes a left-wing viewpoint. They attempt to lead their readers to a certain perspective on political and moral issues. It is widely held that, as long as they are open about what they are doing, there is no harm in this.

Television presents problems where the promotion of views and values is concerned, as it is always possible for those in control of drama, especially widely viewed soap operas, to use them to promote their views. This could be done by slanting story lines in favour of one character who takes the view that the writers want viewers to take. While it is legitimate for dramatists to promote debate on issues (drama is a very effective medium for such discussion) concerns may be raised if certain people hold a privileged position of being able to influence viewers, some of whom may have inadequate critical powers.

There are therefore serious political questions about how such power can be controlled. Clearly, we are all entitled to express our views, but we may feel that allowing certain people and organisations far more power than others have is dangerous for democracy. Society therefore has to ask how such power can be moderated. The moderation that we require is often attempted by:

- controlling the number of newspapers and television channels a person or organisation can own
- establishing a system whereby the media is accountable for its standards
- fostering competition and diversity in the provision and ownership of media.

 The relationship between politicians and the media can work in several ways. While politicians might feel that it is important for there to be controls on media ownership, the media can do a good job of exposing information that politicians want to hide.

The media can be useful and problematic to politicians.

Politicians often seek to manipulate the media to suit their own ends. The means by which they do this is by ensuring that information favourable to them reaches the media, while unfavourable information is kept as secret as possible. They sometimes make sure that unfavourable information that has to be released enters the public domain at the same time as a major story that will distract attention from it. Politicians also attempt to control the image that they present through the media.

Yet in healthy democracies, the media can also act as a brake on the actions of politicians, as it may reveal embarrassing information about them, for example:

- lies, financial misdealings and other crimes they might have committed
- inconsistencies between politicians' public image and their private behaviour
- connections between politicians and powerful business interests seeking to control policy by donating to politicians and their parties
- information that will embarrass governments, such as examples of how policies are failing.

These exposures help to keep democracy healthy, because without information the public would find it hard to hold governments to account.

The media might also campaign on issues that it feels to be important. The *Independent*, for example, argued for the legalisation of cannabis, and campaigned for a powerful freedom of information act that would enable the public to be kept informed about the actions of the government and other powers.

 The media can also create culture. Take the example of soap operas. Magazine and tabloid newspaper publishers have responded to the popularity of these programmes by:

The media has a role in creating culture.

- publishing stories that follow their stars' lives
- reporting forthcoming events in programmes as though they were news.

The result is that the soap operas become a larger part of their followers' lives and a 'soap opera culture' has developed. But the media can only do this because there is a market for this kind of thing, so the culture-creating process is an interaction between the public and the media. Similarly, film and theatre critics can have a large say in whether or not a production is successful and therefore they have a role in forming the culture of their readers. Attitudes to sport may be formed by the views of the pundits of press and television.

The Power of the Media

 At one time there were few cultural outlets, namely several national newspapers and magazines and the radio. Soon television was introduced, but there were few channels. Publishing was rather difficult for individuals, as type-setting and printing costs were quite heavy. Thus those dominating the media were in powerful positions to influence the information reaching the public.

The number of media outlets is greater than it was.

The advent of the Internet, desk-top publishing and a much wider range of television channels has made it far more difficult for powerful people to control information than was previously the case. Anyone with access to the Internet can send information around the world very easily, and a wider range of channels has meant that there is scope for a wider range of views. It is now relatively easy for individuals or smaller organisations to publish a magazine, as typesetting can be done on a home computer.

The result is likely to be felt in closed societies dominated by one political or religious viewpoint, as they will find it harder to prevent information from reaching their people. Only by cutting off electronic communications with the rest of the world can they keep control of information, but in doing so they will cut themselves off from economic contacts and this may lead to their impoverishment and decay.

Reflection

Thus, in a world in which the possession of information is the key to wealth and power, the media has enormous influence, but with the availability of computer technology, control of information is passing out of the hands of big newspapers and television stations and their political allies, and is being shared more widely. This can only be for the public good.

15 minutes

 your knowledge

Read the passage below and answer the questions.

The final period of John Major's government was beset by exposures of the misbehaviour of several ministers and other members of parliament, all of which were ruthlessly exposed by the media. Some were clearly guilty of financial misdemeanours, such as taking cash for asking parliamentary questions, whereas others were found to be involved in sexual scandals. But exposing sexual misdemeanours is controversial, for they are part of an individual's private life, whereas financial misbehaviour is a more public matter. On the one hand, there have been many competent statesmen whose sexual behaviour was less than perfect, and few people are perfect in this area anyway. On the other hand, it is argued that a person who is unfaithful to their spouse in private will be unfaithful to the country under pressure, though there is little or no evidence for this. More strongly argued is the case that the members of a party that proclaimed family values ought to abide by such values. It seems ironic that a person whose company exploits the poor in the underdeveloped world, but is faithful to their spouse, can survive censure, whereas an affair might break the career of an otherwise well-behaved person. But some people claim that politicians are in such an exalted position that we are entitled to expect the highest standards from them and that the press is right to expose them.

 Why, according to the writer, might financial scandals be regarded differently than sexual scandals?

 Sum up the arguments for and against exposing the private lives of politicians.

 Should there be any constraints on the exposure of private lives in the media?

15 minutes

Test your knowledge

1 What is ideology?

2 Ideologies sometimes arise out of _____ _____.
(a) class interest
(b) public relations
(c) childhood background

3 Ideologies promote some _____ more than others.

4 Left-wing ideologies extol _____ more than personal liberty.

5 Right-wing ideologies value _____ property very highly.

6 Does the right–left division satisfactorily account for all political views?

Answers

1 a belief system held for reasons other than ideas alone 2 (a) 3 values
4 equality 5 private 6 no

✔ **If you got them all right, skip to page 40**

Ideology and Values

30 minutes

Improve your knowledge

1. The term ideology is widely used but not as widely understood. It is often used to refer to any belief system, but it denotes a system of belief that is held for reasons other than ideas alone. A belief system held on the strength of its ideas alone is better regarded as a philosophy, though in practice the division between the two is not exact. We might hold a belief system because its ideas are appealing, but we can have other reasons for doing so. We might have not only beliefs about what is politically right and wrong, but also interests that we seek to satisfy. It is not necessarily wrong to have interests or to seek to satisfy them. However, there are problems:

Key points from AS in a Week

Bias
page 27

The term ideology is often loosely used.

- Our interests may be legitimate or illegitimate. For example, a poor person has a legitimate interest in acquiring more money; whereas in eighteenth- and nineteenth-century Britain the landowning classes tried to resist the granting of the vote to poor people, as they felt that their interests would not be served by this reform. This was an illegitimate interest.
- We can deceive ourselves that what is in our interests is right, and in the overall interest of society. It could be argued that self-deception is a universal human defect; and self-interest can distort our views.

Take the example of the issue as to whether the United Kingdom should join the Euro (the single European currency). Tackling the issue on economics alone is not going to work, as people have enormous interests that come into play. For example:

- Ordinary people will benefit as they will not need to pay commission to money changers when they are holidaying in other European countries.
- Those who profit by changing money and speculating in currency will lose much lucrative business, and so may be resolutely opposed to the Euro.
- Many businesses involved in export believe that trading in Euros will enable them to control their costs, and so they are in favour.
- There are people who dislike change and so are against the Euro. A dislike of change is an interest just as the others are, as change is uncomfortable to many people.

A major problem is that ideological interests might mask people's true motives. For example:

- Money speculators might mask their opposition to joining under the façade of patriotism – 'keep the pound'.
- Businesses in favour of joining might claim that the customers will benefit when it is really their own interests that they are seeking.
- Both sides might play down the disadvantages, so as not to weaken their positions.

Ideology can therefore express itself in control of information and in ensuring that only information favourable to a certain view is promulgated.

2 Marxism developed the concept of ideology, as Marx believed that capitalism and any system of belief other than his was based on 'false consciousness', his term for a false understanding of the world. Therefore, other belief systems were ideologies and his was not! Underlying Marx's view is the belief that the interests of the working class were legitimate and therefore should not be regarded as a factor distorting a belief system, whereas the capitalists' interests were illegitimate, destructive and greedy and so should be discounted.

Ideology is a belief system that expresses economic interests.

Marx believed that class interest was behind ideological differences. He saw the world as the interplay of conflicting classes, of which the two dominant ones in his time were the capitalists and the industrial working class, which he called the Proletariat, the leaders of the class struggle. These classes were in the process of absorbing other smaller and less significant classes as the conflict between capital and labour reached its peak. Marx believed that class was the major factor in ideology, as it determined what your interests were, and so ideological differences between capitalist and working classes were the expression of their different interests. In Marx's view, all interests were fundamentally economic and so all ideological differences had an economic foundation. However, the belief that Marxism is not the expression of illegitimate interests can be questioned, because its aspiration that the state should control all means of production offers good opportunities for would-be bureaucrats and politicians. We can suspect some self-interest lurking here.

You should therefore be aware of how self-interest affects people's views.

Ideology and Values

Different
ideologies accept
different values.

3 Different ideologies emphasise different values. There are many values with some relevance to politics, including:

- individual liberty, the freedom to do what you want within limits
- equality, that all are equal in the sight of the state
- justice, that everyone should fairly share the burdens and benefits of social living
- fraternity, the belief that society should involve a shared life for all its citizens
- respect for the environment
- respect for private property
- security.

People hold these values to various degrees, but they are also apt to believe that values have consequences that can be good or bad. They argue, for instance, that justice is not only good, but prevents social unrest; socialists argue that personal economic liberty leads to ill-consequences for society, whereas right-wingers take the opposite view.

Ideologies emphasise some values at the expense of others. Socialists generally play down individual liberty in favour of collective liberty, the rights of the group rather than the individual. Followers of Hayek, a right-wing guru, argue for maximum individual liberty and a minimisation of the state. Similarly, Nozick, a right-wing American philosopher, argues that state services be shrunk to minimum size to leave room for individual liberty to spend your money as you want; whereas others argue that state provision should be widened so as to provide a cohesive society that includes rather than excludes the poor.

Supporters of various ideologies will argue that adoption of their values produces better consequences for society. Socialists, for example, argue that not only is socialism right in itself, but it produces a happier, less divided society than right-wing policies do. Conversely, Thatcherism argued that a happy society would result from the maximisation of individual economic liberty.

Ideology and Values

 Right- and left-wing are misleading terms (although they are commonly used for the sake of brevity), and each of them covers a wide spectrum of political positions.

Left-wing ideologies include socialism, communism of various kinds, and social democracy. The common element in these views is that the state should provide services for its people, and that this means that it should impose some constraints upon economic liberty. The reason for these constraints is that the left generally highlights the suffering caused by capitalism and believes that the only way to prevent it is to constrain it.

Left-wing ideologies believe in state or community control of the economy.

- Communism takes the extreme position of arguing that all economic power should be in state hands and communist countries nationalised all the means of production (factories, farms, etc.).
- Socialists are in favour of a limited amount of nationalisation, and argue for controls on businesses to ensure that they do not damage the community or exploit their workers.
- Social democracy, the position which seems to be held by many in the UK Labour Party, is less interested in controlling economic activity than in providing a social framework in which it can operate fairly. It accepts that the market is beyond government control, but it tries to exercise constraints.

 The term right-wing covers a wide range of positions including:

- authoritarian governments, such as military regimes, which rule in the interests of the capitalists and landowners; these regimes might be termed plutocratic, as power is in the hands of the wealthy
- democratic regimes that emphasise the importance of economic liberty and private enterprise and property, an example of which was the Thatcher government in the UK
- moderate right-wing regimes, such as the Christian Democrats in Germany and some other European countries, which value social cohesion, justice and provision for the poor, along with economic liberty. Christian Democracy has been greatly influenced by Roman Catholic social ethics, which teaches that society should respect the rights of workers, employers and customers.

Right-wing ideologies believe in individual control in economic matters.

The right always places great importance on private property and the right to acquire it by trade or inheritance. It often uses the language of freedom, but this can be deceptive, as certain right-wing regimes minimise the freedom of those who disagree with them, as we saw with the Pinochet government in Chile, between the 1970s and the 1990s.

6 The right–left distinction is a weak one, as there are political positions that do not fall easily into these categories, if at all.

There is a wide range of views between left and right.

- Many people say that they belong to the centre, which emphasises right- and left-wing values.
- Liberal Democrats argue that they are of neither the right nor left, but a radical third choice that breaks free from the conventional capital versus labour, freedom versus equality stereotypes. This third choice involves maximising the exercise of socially responsible freedom, and of public accountability, especially at a local level, where Liberal Democrats believe that power should be exercised.
- The Green movement believes that the right and left wing both place too much importance on the creation of material wealth and neglect the environment. They point out that this materialistic value system is leading the world to disaster and that we must respect the Earth.
- Green ideology is linked to the New Economics, which argues for a radical alternative to capitalism and socialism, in which socially responsible individual and community-based enterprise is encouraged, as opposed to large businesses divorced from the communities that they serve. Like Greens, supporters of this movement tend to be those who have decided that they do not want to be involved in conventional economic activity and want to have a more harmonious relationship with nature and society, while keeping their personal freedom.

Reflection

Ideologies vary in the interests that they represent and in the values that they promote. When responding to a political point you should try to see how ideas, values and interests combine to influence the ways in which people think.

15 minutes

Use your knowledge

Read the passage and answer the questions.

If the Gross National Product of the United Kingdom grew by, say, five per cent – or about £2,000 million a year – could we then use all or most of this money, this additional wealth, to 'fulfil our nation's aspirations'?

Assuredly not; for under private ownership every bit of wealth, as it arises, is immediately and automatically privately appropriated. The public authorities have hardly any income of their own and are reduced to extracting from the pockets of their citizens monies which the citizens consider to be rightfully their own. Not surprisingly, this leads to an endless battle of wits between tax collectors and citizens, in which the rich, with the help of highly paid tax experts, normally do very much better than the poor. In an effort to stop 'loopholes' the tax laws become ever more complicated and the demand for – and therefore the income of – tax consultants becomes ever larger. As the taxpayers feel that something they have earned is being taken away from them, they not only try to exploit every possibility of legal tax avoidance, not to mention practices of illegal tax evasion, they also raise an insistent cry in favour of the curtailment of public expenditure. 'More taxation for more public expenditure' would not be a vote-catching slogan in an election campaign, no matter how glaring may be the discrepancy between private affluence and public squalor.

There is no way out of this dilemma unless the need for public expenditure is recognised in the structure of ownership of the means of production.

It is not merely a question of public squalor, such as the squalor of many mental homes, of prisons, and of countless other publicly maintained services and institutions; this is the negative side of the problem. The positive side arises where large amounts of public funds have been and are being spent on what is generally called the 'infrastructure', and the benefits go largely to private enterprise free of charge. This is well known to anyone who has ever been involved in starting or running an enterprise in a poor society where the 'infrastructure' is insufficiently developed or altogether lacking. He cannot rely on cheap transport and other public services; he may have to provide at his own expense many things which he would obtain free or at small expense in a society with a highly developed infrastructure; he cannot count on being able to recruit trained people: he has to train them himself; and so on. All the educational, medical, and research institutions in any society, whether rich or poor, bestow incalculable benefits upon private enterprise – benefits for which private enterprise does not pay directly as a matter of course, but only indirectly by way of taxes, which, as already mentioned, are resisted, resented, campaigned against, and often skilfully avoided.

(From *Small is Beautiful* by EF Schumacher)

1 The author identifies a conflict between state and citizens. What is it?

2 Why are the rich advantaged in this conflict?

3 Summarise the problems suffered by people starting up businesses in underdeveloped societies, according to this passage.

4 Why might the author's attitudes be considered somewhat left-wing?

15 minutes

Test your knowledge

1. What is a constitution?

2. What is proportional representation?

3. What is the role of a government?

4. European law is made by ___ _____ __ _____.

5. Why is local government important?

6. What is civil society?

Answers

1 a set of rules enacting how politics will proceed in a country 2 an electoral system that awards seats in legislatures in proportion to the votes cast 3 to rule the country in accordance with the law 4 the Council of Ministers 5 It enables people to govern themselves using local knowledge. 6 a layer of society between individuals and governments

✓ **If you got them all right, skip to page 48**

Political Processes

30 minutes

Improve your knowledge

You may be aware that many people in the United Kingdom want the country to have a written constitution like the one enjoyed by the United States. But what is a constitution and what does it do?

The idea of a constitution was first put forward in England in the eighteenth century, when notable thinkers came to the conclusion that governments should work under a set of rules that prescribed what they could and could not do. This was to prevent them from overriding human rights and oppressing the people. The idea was exported to the United States, where it became the foundation of the American political system. It specifies certain rights that all citizens possess and the powers that each part of the American political establishment can have. There is also a Supreme Court that can rule on whether the constitution has been breached.

A constitution is a set of rules specifying how a society is governed.

While the United Kingdom has no written constitution, it is generally accepted that it has an unwritten one, a set of parliamentary customs that acts as a constitution but whose unwritten character provides flexibility. Supporters of a written constitution argue that an unwritten constitution provides no guarantee against unjust governments that deny rights. However, the European Declaration on Human Rights, which the UK is signed up to, acts in some way like a constitution, as it guarantees citizens' rights against governments. It is worth considering this issue for yourself.

One of the issues of our time is whether or not the United Kingdom should adopt proportional representation at national and local elections. The problem lies in the mismatch between votes cast and seats gained in UK elections. The general principle of democratic government is that the proportion of votes cast for a party should roughly be represented in the seats that it obtains; but this has not been so in UK elections for many years, as it works only when there are two parties and not when there are many. The UK uses the 'first past the post' system, in which the candidate with most votes wins the seat, even though the total cast for other candidates added together might be greater than those cast for the winner.

Proportional representation attempts to balance the representation a party gets with the number of votes it received.

The issue has become more topical because the Scottish, Welsh and Northern Irish assemblies are elected by proportional representation, in which the voting system awards seats in relation to votes cast.

Defenders of the existing system argue that it was designed to produce strong government and that if we had proportional representation we might have weak coalition governments (involving pacts between parties), as found in Italy, for example. They also argue that the electors could not know the outcome of voting for a particular party because they would not know which parties would be in coalition. Supporters of change argue that countries such as Germany have had proportional representation since the Second World War and have done rather well under it. They also argue that not having a single dominant party prevents politicians from the dominant party from doing whatever they please while in office. It is also pointed out that the British system was not designed to produce strong government, but just evolved over the years.

There are several systems of proportional representation. The system used in the elections for the London Assembly involves individual candidates being elected and a top-up procedure by which inequalities in party representation are eradicated by topping up from a party list, so that there is roughly proportional representation. A question to ask yourself is whether the United Kingdom should have proportional representation for all elections or whether it should keep the current system.

3 Many people are unclear about the role of government. Government does not make laws – parliament (the legislature) does. This confusion arises in many countries because the government is drawn from members of national parliaments, as is the case in the UK, where the prime minister is the leader of the largest party in parliament. It need not be the case that all members of the government are members of the House of Commons or the Lords, and it is even possible in theory for the prime minister to be a member of neither, though this does not occur in practice.

Governments do not make laws, they apply them.

Governments run the state, and they must act according to the law. Thus, although we hear government ministers argue that they are going to change the law, they must ask parliament to do so.

A major area of concern in the United Kingdom and the western world in general is the way in which governments can push their policies through parliament using the party disciplinary machinery. Members can be subject to the discipline of their party 'whips', who can recommend those who comply with their leader's instructions for promotion, or ultimately withdraw the whip from rebel members, effectively expelling them from the party and reselection as a candidate at the next election. Many people feel that this system is bad for democracy, as it prevents some members of parliament from speaking their minds. Is this diminishing of parliament a real problem in your opinion, and if so, what can and should be done about it?

 There is intense debate in the United Kingdom about the role of the European Union in the government of this country. There are several broad views on the issue:

- The UK is a nation that should be in charge of its own affairs and not be subject to laws made by other countries.
- In the modern world, the idea of a totally independent nation state is losing its meaning; we need to be part of a bigger unit so that we can effectively manage our affairs. We should therefore become part of a union of sovereign states.
- The concept of the nation state is no longer relevant, so we should become part of a European superstate. This latter view is not commonly held.

The UK shares in the government of the European Union.

The idea that the European Union involves foreigners 'telling us what to do' is a misrepresentation of what happens in Europe. The UK has a share in the government of Europe and can influence what happens in other states, just as it can influence what happens within its borders. This influence is effected through certain democratic institutions:

- the Council of Ministers, which consists of ministers from all countries in the EU – for example, if there is an environmental problem, the council of ministers will consist of environmental ministers from all countries
- the European Parliament, whose main power is to advise the Council of Ministers and supervise the European Commission, the powerful European civil service.

The issue is how much power any nation should concede to the European institutions. The principle of subsidiarity is important:

- All rules should be made at the lowest level compatible with effective government.

Thus, if a rule only applies to England, it should not be made in Europe, and a rule that applies to Manchester should be made by the council in that city. However, some rules have a European scope, and they should be made by European institutions.

Ultimately, your own attitude to the European issue will be determined by the importance that you place on the nation state. If you see it as a self-contained body totally sovereign over itself, then European influence will be seen as depriving it of its rightful sovereignty. If you believe that the world is one community that should be governed at various levels, ranging from parish councils to the United Nations, you will be more ready to accept European influence in national affairs. Supporters of this latter view point out that nation states cannot alone cope with the great multinational companies, which can move money and jobs around the world at will, out of the control of governments, and that only powerful transnational institutions can cope with them. How much power over British decisions should in your opinion be exercised by the European Union?

5 It is generally agreed that healthy democracies should have effective local government. The reason for this is that if decisions in Inverness, for example, were made by a politician or civil servant in London, it is unlikely that they would be made by a person who knew local conditions or was aware of what local people wanted. Furthermore, it would be hard to influence a person several hundred miles away, and still harder to remove them if they made decisions that the people of Inverness did not like. Having decisions made by local councillors who know local people and conditions, and who can be removed by the local electorate, means that local people can run their own communities. It enables them to participate in government in a way that would be impossible if decisions were made by distant figures in the national capital. Yet there is a problem that it is hard to get people to take part in local democracy, probably because of the amount of work involved.

Local government is necessary to a well run society.

How in your opinion can local democracy in the UK be invigorated?

6

Civic society is a layer between government and individuals. It is composed of charities, churches, friendly societies, trades unions and so on. There is increasing interest in the importance of this layer of society, which declined between pressures from a swelling of state power on one hand and the growth of individualism and consumerism on the other. There has been a decline in participation in such institutions, as we see from the slippage in church attendance, which has declined along with involvment in all participatory organisations like those mentioned above. This decline may be due to the following problems:

There is a layer of society between state and individual.

- British people work longer hours than any other people in Europe and consequently have less time to devote to voluntary activities than they might like.
- The amount of debt into which people have fallen makes them work excessively to pay it off.
- There are many entertainments available to distract people from less amusing, but socially valuable pursuits.

Yet those who support the reinvigoration of civic society argue that it is organisations such as those above that can help people participate in running their lives and can act as a bridge between the state and the individual. It spreads power around the community rather than concentrating it in the hands of politicians.

Ask yourself whether the development of civic society should be encouraged and, if so, how this could be achieved.

15 minutes

 **your knowledge**

Read the following passage and answer the questions.

The problem facing the United Kingdom faces all democracies: how to encourage participation in the political process. Societies have developed a class of professional politicians, who are assisted by party activists, but beyond this political class there is a worrying decline in the numbers of people who play any part in political life. The pressures of work and family can be very demanding, and people can become too tired to do other things. Entertainment provides an option which is much more attractive than voluntary work. The problem covers the whole range of voluntary activity, with participation declining in favour of television watching. Perhaps the growth of individualism has been a factor, as people do not feel that they want to join in with others and would rather 'do their own thing'. Perhaps the solution is to encourage smaller units of government, with the large metropolitan councils devolving powers down to smaller, local units. We might also encourage participation in civic organisations, such as trades unions. Perhaps we need to discourage debt, which makes people work excessively to pay it off. Above all, we need to encourage a sense that we are members of a society, that it belongs to us and that we are responsible for running it.

1 Why does the author think that participation is declining?

2 Why do you think that the author believes this decline to be a matter for concern?

3 Why do you think individualism might be a factor in the decline of participation?

4 The author believes that power ought to be devolved downwards from large councils to smaller, local units. Do you think that this solution would facilitate participation?

Explanation and Behaviour

15 minutes

Test your knowledge

1 The area of learning that tries to explain behaviour by reference to what is going on in human minds is _____.

2 Which of the following tries to explain human behaviour by reference to hidden thoughts and motives?
(a) psychoanalysis
(b) psychometrics
(c) psychotherapy

3 The area of learning that tries to explain behaviour in terms of influences from society is _____.

4 What is economics?

5 Why is it impossible for any single subject to explain behaviour fully?

Answers

1 psychology 2 psychoanalysis 3 sociology 4 the study of money and how it affects behaviour 5 because humans are influenced by both external and internal factors

 If you got them all right, skip to page 55

Explanation and Behaviour

30 minutes

Improve your knowledge

Read the following passage.

It appears that all people are motivated by the need for self-esteem. Each of us has a self-concept or self-image, and we would like it to be as positive as possible. If we receive praise our self-image becomes positive, and we are more confident because of it. Blame or negative stimuli have the opposite effect. We lose confidence and can even cease to value ourselves. Many personality problems and mental difficulties arise from low self-esteem, so therapy involves identifying the factors which have produced this negative self-image and correcting them.

> **Key points from AS in a Week**
>
> Different Kinds of Knowledge
> pages 12–15

This passage explains human behaviour in terms of an idea that it assumes is relevant to all human minds. As it focuses on internal, mental factors, it is a psychological explanation. All explanations of the psychological kind involve identifying the factors that shape human behaviour, such as:

* Psychology deals with the human mind.

* ideas and beliefs
* attitudes
* feelings and emotions
* values and goals
* abilities
* ways of perceiving the world and the limitations on our senses.

The problem is that the theory behind the passage above is not necessarily correct. It probably has some truth, but it is not a complete explanation of behaviour, as other theories may have something valuable to contribute. This particular theory overlooks the importance of drives, such as the sex drive, urge for knowledge and so on, and it overlooks our concern for others, assuming that we are all self-centred.

So if, in your examination, you have to respond to a passage explaining human behaviour, be aware that you can draw on psychological concepts, but also that there may be several ways of explaining the behaviour concerned.

Explanation and Behaviour

2 Psychoanalytic explanations are common, but they are often criticised. Read the passage below for an example of one.

Psychoanalysis attempts to uncover hidden motives.

> *When you dreamt that you were killing a monster you were really expressing a desire to kill your father. Since childhood you have resented him because of his hold on your mother's affections, which you wanted all for yourself. But you feel guilty about hating your father, so symbolically you turn him into a monster and kill him that way. Only through symbolically killing him can you release the tension which has been tormenting you. Of course you will deny wanting to kill your father, but you are merely refusing to accept the truth, so this confirms that you feel guilty about your desire and are covering it up.*

This is a fictional example of a psychoanalytic explanation, based on Freud's (the founder of psychoanalysis) theory of the Oedipus [pronounced *ee dip uss*] complex, which refers to a boy's unconscious desire to kill his father and possess his mother. Freud believed that this repressed desire was common to all men.

There are several problems with this kind of explanation:

- How does the speaker know what is hidden in the mind of the person to whom he is speaking?
- How does he know that this Oedipus complex is found in all minds?
- Psychoanalysis rests on the assumption that what is hidden has more explanatory value than what is obvious and apparent. Thus what we think about ourselves is less important than our hidden desires. This assumption is open to challenge.
- If a client denies the existence in themselves of certain desires and emotions, the psychoanalyst will suggest that this implies that they exist but are repressed. Philosophers argue that the weakness of such circular arguments is that they cannot be falsified, and so they cannot ever be proved true.

However, many people would argue that there is value in psychoanalytic explanation, as it may identify hidden urges and thoughts and uncover the self-deceptions that we all practise. Those in favour of psychoanalysis believe that it is only through examining our deepest fears and desires that we can come to an understanding of ourselves.

Like all explanations of behaviour, psychoanalytic explanations should be critically examined.

Explanation and Behaviour

 The sociological explanation is very popular, as sociology is a much studied subject. Read the following passage.

Sociology studies the effects of society on behaviour.

> *Football hooliganism is no longer the preserve of the working classes, the traditional stereotype of the hooligan. Hooligans can be found in middle and upper classes – there are some well-heeled professionals who have been involved. Yet this should not surprise us, as rowdy behaviour has always been associated with young aristocrats, as the history of the eighteenth century shows. In its earliest stages, football hooliganism may have been associated with a desire to participate in the club, a desire which is frustrated as it is only possible to be a spectator, leading some fans to engage in fighting with other fans. It may also derive from a sense that one's masculine identity has to be proved in battle, an opportunity denied to many young males in an age when most men do not fight in wars.*

Note that sociologists base their arguments upon statistics, which show them what is happening in society rather than what people think is happening (although statistics can be misleading and investigators using them can overlook major trends). Sociological explanation tries to set behaviour in a social context. You can see how the writer of this passage sets hooliganism in the context of:

- the lack of opportunities for young males to participate in the activities of their chosen club, when it is participation that they all desire
- the lack of opportunities nowadays for proving one's manhood in battle
- the general problem of aggression by young males.

Note, though, that the writer could not avoid talking about human motives, the field of psychology, as it is these motives that make us respond to our environment. However, sociology does not involve in-depth analysis of motives, which is the task of psychology.

When dealing with explanations of behaviour, it is important that you identify the social context in which behaviour occurs and to which it responds.

Explanation and Behaviour

 4 Economic explanation

Read the following passage.

Economics studies money and how it affects and is affected by behaviour.

> *Calculations show that the market for Internet book-selling is likely to decline before levelling out at a stable 15% of the market. Despite initial optimism that the World Wide Web would soon force traditional stores to close, events in the market show that this is not happening and the traditional stores are surviving, albeit with a small decline in profits. This may be due to downsizing, and to the fact that not everyone has access to a computer whenever they want it and so cannot buy from Internet booksellers. It may also be relevant that customers can visit high-street booksellers as part of a shopping trip, which they cannot do with the Internet. Competition from existing mail order booksellers can be quite strong, and so it is unlikely that the ambitious predictions for Internet book selling will be realised.*

You can see that economic explanation is quite complex. It involves trying to explain the behaviour of money and the way in which people behave in relation to it. Economic explanation includes the following elements:

- mathematics – economists use complex calculations to enable them to predict future economic events (although economic predictions have a poor rate of success, and economists are constantly trying to improve their calculations)
- identifying and quantifying factors that influence economic affairs
- assumptions about what motivates people, although these assumptions can be wrong.

The sheer difficulties of economic explanation arise from the fact that it is attempting to deal with the enormously complex subject of the economic choices made by billions of people. If we accept that there is any element of freedom and personal choice in behaviour, it is essentially unpredictable. Furthermore, people are responsive to predictions. For example, if economists predict that there will be massive demand for fuel in December, people stock up or economise, so the demand is not what is predicted.

So economic predictions should be treated with some caution, although there are factors that can be seen to influence economic behaviour. Despite this, we cannot predict with absolute accuracy what people will do.

Explanation and Behaviour

 5 The insufficiency of all single subject explanations

No single subject can explain behaviour.

Read the following passage.

> *The increase in the status of women throughout the twentieth century was due to a number of factors. Clearly, the simple fact that women could do the kind of work that was once exclusive to men showed people that they had more capacities than many had thought. Getting women into paid employment became important for a society that wanted to expand production to augment its wealth. So the ideal of the working woman was actively promoted. Yet women saw that going to work could give them economic independence and raise them above the semi-servile state in which they had long lived. In a society in which a person was valued according to their career success and wealth accrued, women felt that self-esteem could only be gained from having careers. As the desire for self-esteem is the basic human motive, women chose careers as the most effective way to obtain it.*

Note that this explanation draws on a number of elements:

- Psychological. It explains women's behaviour in terms of the self-esteem theory.
- Sociological. It shows how women's roles changed because of changes in society.
- Economic. The writer identifies the desire for economic independence as an explanation of women's behaviour. This includes a strong psychological element.

You should try to incorporate a variety of elements in any explanation of human behaviour.

Explanation and Behaviour

15 minutes

Use your knowledge

Read the following passage and answer the questions.

A career is a job in which there is an expectation of advancement in wealth, power and status. In fact, the reason for opting for a career rather than a job is that you feel that advancing in wealth, power and status is likely to make you more happy. People who are successful in their careers are likely to be people who value the advancement that careers can bring and work hard to attain their goals. Before the Second World War, few people could seriously envisage having a career, but, as economies expanded, opportunities were created and careers became more available. Ambitious young people saw opportunities that their parents did not have. Behind the encouragement of careers were economic interests that wanted to encourage harder work, so rather than being a personal choice, careerism came to be presented as an obligation. Anyone who said that he or she just wanted a job would be despised as unaspiring and lazy. Yet there have been reactions against this career culture. The hippies fought against it, and some young people now question the tyranny that careers seem to have over their lives. They remember the old adage, 'you work to live, not live to work'.

1 What, according to the author, are the ideas and motives behind a desire to have a career?

2 What economic factors have influenced young people to aspire to have a career?

3 The author describes a career culture. What are the characteristics of this culture?

4 Why might the hippies have reacted against the 'tyranny of careers'?

15 minutes

Test your knowledge

1 One theory that evaluates actions by their consequences is:
(a) human rights theory
(b) utilitarianism
(c) prescriptivism

2 Many ethical theories like to identify the proper _____ of human activity.

3 Immanuel Kant believed that persons were _____ in themselves.

4 Freedoms that cannot be taken away from us are called:
(a) rights
(b) duties
(c) fortunes

5 What is known as the first virtue of society?
(a) happiness
(b) luck
(c) justice

6 In complex situations we must make moral _____.

Answers

1 (a) 2 goal 3 ends 4 (a) 5 (c) 6 judgments

 If you got them all right, skip to page 62

Ethical Issues

30 minutes

Improve your knowledge

1 Consider this scenario. You are working in a hospital in the developing world, and only have one dose of medicine left, but there are two people who can benefit from it. They are the widowed mother of a young family and an unmarried and childless nurse from the hospital at which you work. Both are equally ill and both are the same age, but to which one do you give the medicine?

Key points from AS in a Week

Moral Responsibility pages 68–70

This is a sad dilemma, and there is no easy way of resolving it. We might make this decision by working out the consequences of each course of action:

- The nurse might save many lives, but workers can be replaced.
- The mother has fewer dependents on her than the nurse has, but they depend more deeply on her than the nurse's patients do.

Utilitarians believe in the greatest happiness of the greatest number.

Utilitarians assess all actions by their consequences, specifically by the happiness that accrues from them.

- Act utilitarians assess every single act as far as they can, however difficult this may be.
- Rule utilitarians believe that following certain basic rules leads to the best consequences.
- Consequences can be for yourself and others, and they can be physical or mental.

The principle that utilitarians follow is 'the way that leads to the greatest happiness of the greatest number should be chosen'. You do not need to be a utilitarian to take consequences into account, but utilitarianism is a useful way of showing how to consider consequences.

When making ethical decisions we need to take into account the consequences of the actions that we make.

2 Having a goal is very important for ethical theories, as your goals will specify where your actions are leading. Quite simply, it is necessary to know where you are going.

Consequences must be taken into account in ethical decision making.

Ethical theories vary in the goals which they prescribe:

- Utilitarianism specifies that the goal is happiness.
- The goal of many religious ethics is to please God and achieve eternal life in heaven.
- Some people might say that their goal is self-fulfilment.
- Marxists had the goal of creating a perfect communist society.

Most ethical theories hold that happiness will come about from people reaching their goal, but:

- they differ in how they think happiness can be obtained
- they may differ in whether they think happiness is for all or just some; for example, there are some religious groups who believe that only a few will achieve the happiness of heaven
- they may differ in where and when their goal is to be obtained, whether it is in the present or the future.

These differences are very significant, as they determine the courses of action that those who hold them will adopt.

Thus, if you are discussing ethical issues, ensure that you have thought through the goal or state of affairs that you are aiming to attain and how ethical activity will help you in this.

3 Consider the following passage.

Slavery involves using a person as a tool for your own ends. Its modern relatives are those economic systems that treat some people as if they did not matter: workers are regarded as items of equipment to be discarded, whose rights are a nuisance to employers; the poor in developing lands are regarded as easy material for exploitation, their rights are overridden and their lands exploited and damaged by the great multinational companies.

We must not treat persons as means to an end.

Ethical Issues

The author of this passage is identifying an ethical problem, that people are often treated as though they did not matter. They are regarded as tools to another person's ends, not ends in themselves. If we regard persons as means to our ends, we use them with no regard for their well-being; if we regard them as ends in themselves, we must respect them and their needs.

Immanuel Kant stated that all persons are ends in themselves. This means that there are things that we cannot do to them. We cannot treat them in ways that do not respect them.

We might say that certain actions or states of affairs are good in themselves:

- If someone asked what is the use of being happy, we would think them somewhat misled, as happiness does not need to be useful – it is an end in itself.
- Similarly, to ask what use is love is to beg the question of whether or not love has any purpose other than itself. If love serves an ulterior motive it is not love.
- Religious people argue that praying and relating to God does not need any purpose, it is simply good in itself.

When you are taking part in any ethical discussion, remember the theory that persons are ends in themselves and that their happiness and the love that we give them or they give others does not need any justification.

 Any ethical discussion can turn to talk of rights. Rights are certain freedoms that belong to persons, and which we cannot take away without extremely good reasons, if at all. For example, freedom of conscience is a fundamental right, although we do not allow persons to practise beliefs which involve taking away the rights of others. Freedom in general is a right, though it might be limited by the state for reasons of good order or of appropriate punishment. Rights might be taken away for good reasons by appropriate authorities, but individuals have no right to take them away.

Ethics says that we must respect rights.

Rights are side-constraints on the actions that we perform. This means that when we are deciding what to do in any situation we must consider what are the rights of the persons involved and we must produce a strategy that will respect all the rights concerned.

There is a hierarchy of rights and freedoms, some being more important than others. For example, the right to life is very high on the agenda, and freedom of conscience is one of the highest. Thus, the right to life possessed by all people is higher than any individual's right to drive fast through a residential area, so the state imposes limits on a lower freedom to protect a higher one.

In any ethical discussion, respect for rights is very important and all rights must be respected, not a selected few. It is important to be clear which rights and freedoms are more important.

5 Justice is the principle that everyone is entitled to a fair share of the burdens and benefits that accrue from living in society. These are called social goods. They are opposed to natural goods, such as good looks, height, strength and so on.

Justice is the principle on which society rests.

Generally we feel that everyone is entitled to equal shares of certain goods. Thus we all have a right to vote, and no-one now has a right to more than one vote. We all have equal responsibilities as well, for example we must all obey the law.

However, sometimes we give certain people a greater share of social goods or priority in access to them. This can be quite just. For example, you may have been waiting in the accident and emergency branch of a hospital with a minor injury, while a person who arrived after you, but has a very serious injury, will be treated first. This is quite just and fair, because their needs are higher than yours. One day, in similar conditions, you might benefit from priority of this kind. The treatment is different, but the same rules apply to everyone.

Similarly, society might impose some very heavy responsibilities upon one group of people, for example, those who enforce the law, but it ought to reward them accordingly with privileges or financial benefits.

Respect for rights is an important part of justice. You cannot be treating people justly if you do not respect their rights.

When discussing any ethical situation you should ask what are the requirements of justice in this situation.

Ethical Issues

6 Much ethical discussion comes down to making judgments. Some cases are so clear that no discussion is needed. For example, rape is wrong and there is no justification for it. However, many cases can be quite complex, and there can be serious differences of opinion about what ought to be done. These might include:

Ethical judgments must take into account all relevant considerations.

- problems about the prioritisation of resources
- medical emergencies
- decisions about war and peace.

In all such situations you can only make an ethical decision if you consider:

- the persons involved in the situation
- their rights
- their needs, which might determine who should get priority or special treatment
- the consequences of the various courses of action (although actions/states that are good in themselves, such as happiness, do not need consequences to justify them)
- the degree of certainty that the various consequences have of occurring.

In the end you must:

- weigh them all up
- work out the strategy by which you can produce the best results overall.

15 minutes

 **your knowledge**

Read the passage and answer the questions.

> *There must be certain constraints on the right of free speech. We have set a precedent by banning racially inflammatory material, but perhaps we ought to go further and ban Holocaust denial, the claim that the Nazi genocide of the Jews and others did not happen. Clearly, this is such a stupid view that there is no justification for holding it, so there is no harm in banning it. Those who hold this view are apologists for Hitler, so they serve Hitler's cause by undermining our efforts to prevent anything like the Holocaust from happening again. Yes, we know that John Stuart Mill argued that free speech was essential and that false views would be proved wrong in the crucible of debate, but we cannot trust people to come to the right conclusions. So it is important to ban Holocaust denial.*

1 Summarise the author's reasons for wanting to ban holocaust denial.

2 Can you think of any objections to the author's proposal that Holocaust denial be banned?

3 Write a paragraph in which you argue the case for or against banning Holocaust denial. (Use between 50 and 100 words.)

15 minutes

Test your knowledge

1 Space and time are:
(a) absolute
(b) relative

2 'Science can lead us beyond the origins of the universe.' True or false?

3 'We can observe particles without having any effect on them.' True or false?

4 Which of these thinkers believe that there is no such thing as consciousness?
(a) logical behaviourists
(b) cosmologists
(c) physicists

5 'All scientists agree that mind is purely material.' True or false?

6 'The theory of evolution has not yet answered every question about life on Earth.' True or false?

Answers

1 (b) 2 false 3 false 4 logical behaviourists 5 false 6 true

✔ **If you got them all right, skip to page 69**

Nature of Reality

30 minutes

Improve your knowledge

1 One of the greatest discoveries of the twentieth century was the theory of relativity. It was first put forward by Einstein and published in 1905. His great discovery was that motion, space and time are relative, not absolute. Prior to Einstein many scientists had thought that space and time were absolute and that even if we went outside the universe there would still be space and time, as there is in this world.

Key points from AS in a Week

Science and the Nature of the Universe
pages 58–60

Einstein realised that space and time were not absolute, and that therefore motion could not be absolute. Consider this example. You are sitting in a stationary car and the car next to you moves forward. You have the impression that your car is going backwards. This is because we need to judge motion against a fixed reference point. On Earth we do this in relation to houses, trees, etc., which we know do not move, but in space there is no fixed reference point by which we can judge motion. So all motion is relative.

Time and space are relative, not absolute.

This led to one of Einstein's greatest discoveries, that time is relative too. It seems that time can speed up or slow down, depending on how fast you travel. At the speeds at which we move on Earth the change is vanishingly small, but as objects approach the speed of light, time slows down. This means that, in theory, space travellers should age slower than their fellows on Earth.

The implications of the theory of relativity are far reaching, and it has had a great effect on how scientists carry out their calculations about the movement of objects in space and about how they understand the subatomic (smaller than the atom) world.

2 Science has made enormous strides in its understanding of the beginnings of the universe. Scientists have calculated what the universe was like within a few millionths of a second after the Big Bang (an event that scientists believe took place 10,000 million years ago, in which all the matter of the universe, packed into a small superdense mass, was hurled in all directions by a cataclysmic explosion, creating galaxies and stars). But we have not understood the actual moment of the Big Bang yet. Some scientists are confident that mathematics can take us there, but others are not sure. Even if our calculations reach the Big

It is hard to say whether there was anything before the Big Bang.

Bang itself, we will still have no ability to go beyond it, as science confines itself to the observable universe, and cannot speak of what happened 'before' the Big Bang.

The word 'before' is a problem word, because many thinkers doubt that there was any time before the Big Bang occurred, because the time that we know is relative to this world and does not exist outside it. How can we speak of 'before' when there is no time? It is possible to ask whether the universe is wrapped up in a wider time scale, in which the word 'before' would then be meaningful, but there is no way of knowing this. If there is, however, a succession of worlds coming to be and decaying, as the Hindus believe there is, then there would be some meaning for time outside of this universe. But we do not know whether there is such a succession of worlds.

Many thinkers believe that we cannot speak meaningfully about what is before or beyond the universe, and so there is no point in doing so, a belief that has led some thinkers to argue that we cannot speak meaningfully about God. Religious thinkers believe that they can speak meaningfully about God, who is outside space and time, only because he has crossed the barrier and made himself known in space and time.

3 One very strange discovery that has opened up new vistas in physics is that the observer has an influence on the observed. Psychologists had long recognised that this was the case, as people behave differently when they are observed from when they are in private. The only way in which to observe people is to ensure that they do not know that they are being observed, otherwise they take the observer into account when deciding what to do. While this principle clearly applies when studying humans and probably some animals, scientists had always believed that it did not apply to physics, where you could observe a reality without having any effect on it. But scientists working with subatomic particles have found out that, even in physics, the observer has an effect on what is observed. This raises some interesting questions:

Physics has opened up a strange world to us.

- How does this happen?
- Can we ever really understand the world if we cannot perform experiments in which we have no effect on what is observed?
- What part does consciousness play in the world?

Some scientists and philosophers believe that we ought to change the way in which we look at the world. There are two broad views in competition:

- The majority view at the moment is that the universe is composed of inanimate, unconscious matter, and that consciousness is either nonexistent (a minority view) or a development at some spots in an otherwise lifeless universe.
- More recently, some scientists have argued that consciousness fills the universe, and that mind rather than matter should be regarded as the prime stuff of the universe. This is a still a minority view.

4 This leads us to the discussion of consciousness. Logical behaviourists believe that there is no inner world in the human mind, as it were, and that all human thoughts and emotions can be reduced to observable behaviour that can be studied by scientists. However, there are aspects of our mental lives that cannot be explained behaviourally:

No one has yet explained consciousness.

- qualia: our emotions, sense of colour, etc.
- dispositions to act in certain ways, which cannot be exhaustively described in behavioural terms
- our sense of being conscious, which defies being reduced to a form of physical behaviour.

Scientists and philosophers do not agree about the nature of consciousness, and there is much discussion on the matter. Many believe that it is still a mystery. There are several views:

- One American book was entitled *Consciousness Explained* and it represented the view that science and philosophy could already understand consciousness.
- We have not explained consciousness yet, but science is on the way to doing so.
- Consciousness might be explained, but not by science, which does not have the methods to do so, because it can only observe outward behaviour.
- Consciousness will never be explained. How do the adherents of this view know this?

Nature of Reality

5 Any discussion of consciousness leads us to the tricky question of the relationship between mind and body. There are several competing views:

- The mind is simply the brain. Consciousness is an illusion. The problem is that we know that we are conscious.
- The mind is the brain, but there is a consciousness that exists within it, though it is powerless to control behaviour. The question is, why did it evolve if it exerts no controlling function?
- Humans are a mix of two substances, mind and matter, and the two interrelate. There are several versions of this theory, but the problem is discovering how matter and mind influence each other. Any theory that there is a human soul belongs to this class of views.
- The Hindu view is that humans are primarily a consciousness that 'wraps matter around it'. This view sits uneasily with traditional western science, which emphasises matter, but it has some adherents in the western world, especially amongst those thinkers who regard consciousness as a characteristic of the whole universe.
- Matter is illusory and all is mind. This view has some adherents, but it is not commonly held by western thinkers at the moment. However, some eastern thinkers believe it.

The relationship between mind and body is still a mystery.

6 The theory of evolution plays an important role in science, as it charts the development of life from simple to complex forms. However, it is not free of problems, and scientists have much work to do to deepen our understanding of it. There are several views on evolution:

- Evolution is a fact, and there can be no argument on the matter.
- Evolution is a very well justified theory with no credible rivals.
- Creation scientists, who are fundamentalist Protestants, mostly from America, argue that science disproves evolution and that the biblical account of creation is the correct one.

Evolution is a well justified theory with no credible rivals.

Creation science cannot explain scientific data that suggest that the world is older than the Bible says it is. Its real problem is that it is only necessary for those who take the Bible absolutely literally. Those who do not take it literally have no need of creation science.

However, evolution is not a proven fact, as we can never prove with absolute certainty that anything happened in times before our experience. For it to be a fact, we would have to be able to observe every stage in the evolutionary process, which is impossible. But it is a theory:

- whose only rival, creation science, cannot be taken seriously, and which has no other conceivable rivals
- which fits all the data
- which works as an explanation for the development of life.

Nevertheless, there are problems to be solved in our understanding of evolution:

- Do we know all the factors operating in the evolutionary process? Natural selection is the important one, but could there be others?
- How can we explain the development of the conscious mind from unconscious matter?
- Was there a role for chance in the evolutionary process, and/or could a conscious mind (God, if you want to use the term) have been exerting an influence?

Reflections

The key issue here is what role there is for consciousness in our understanding of the universe. Is the universe and all that is in it inanimate matter, or is consciousness an essential part of things? How you answer this question affects your view of who you are – whether you are just matter, or whether you have a conscious mind and/or soul, and if so, whether there is an afterlife. These questions are likely to affect how you live your life.

15 minutes

Use your knowledge

Read the passage and answer the questions.

The Puzzle of Chance

The standard Darwinian account perceives a twofold intervention of chance in the evolutionary process: first, by bringing forth mutations in the genome, and then by exposing the mutant organisms to an environment in which they could survive. Some investigators, such as Richard Dawkins, appear perfectly satisfied with this twofold element of chance. According to Dawkins, the evolution of the gene pool occurs through trial and error, so that the evolution of living species resembles the work of a 'blind watchmaker'. Given sufficient time, evolution's trials and errors will generate all the living forms that have ever populated the biosphere.

Other scientists are less convinced. An outspoken critic of Darwinism, Michael Denton, asked whether random processes could have constructed an evolutionary sequence of which even a basic element, such as a protein or a gene, is complex beyond human capacities. Can one account statistically for the chance emergence of systems of truly great complexity, such as the mammalian brain when, if specifically organised, just 1 percent of the connections in such a brain would be larger than the connections in the world's entire communications network? Denton concluded that chance mutations acted on by natural selection could well account for variations **within** given species, but hardly for successive variations **among** them.

('Genome' means a set of genes. 'Biosphere' means an area where life is possible.)

(From *The Whispering Pond*, by Ervin Laszlo)

1 Explain in your own words the standard Darwinian account of evolution.

2 What does Richard Dawkins mean by the phrase 'the blind watchmaker'?

3 Why does Michael Denton have reservations about Richard Dawkins' views?

Moral Responsibility

15 minutes

Test your knowledge

1 Science is:
(a) always good
(b) always bad
(c) morally neutral
(d) good but can be misused

2 'The way in which people use scientific discoveries is not the business of scientists.' True or false?

3 'Scientific experiments have no room for ethical concerns.' True or false?

4 'The greenhouse effect is not the result of science.'
(a) true
(b) false
(c) partly true

5 'The environmental problems faced by humanity cannot be solved by science alone.' True or false?

Answers

1 (d) 2 false 3 false 4 partly true 5 true

 If you got them all right, skip to page 76

Moral Responsibility

30 minutes

Improve your knowledge

1 Humans benefit from knowing rather than being ignorant, and so in general there is good reason for them to have a grasp of science, and the deeper the grasp, the better. We can think of several reasons why a knowledge of science is a good thing:

Key points from AS in a Week
Moral Responsibility pages 68–70

- It helps us to solve problems that we encounter in our daily and working lives.
- It helps us to design machines that can improve our quality of life.
- It contributes to medicine and therefore leads to improvements in health.
- Through science we can come to an understanding of our world.

Yet science is not always an unqualified good, because it can be used in harmful ways. For example:

Knowledge can be used or misused.

- Misused scientific knowledge gave Hitler gas chambers and enabled the Gestapo to discover how to inflict maximum pain when torturing victims.
- Scientific knowledge was used to create atomic, chemical and germ weapons.
- While science can be used to serve human need, it can often serve human greed. Industry in developed countries can use scientific skills to swallow up scarce resources to make luxury items while people in poorer countries are going short.
- The technological power that science gives to those countries that possess it can be used to dominate smaller and weaker countries.
- Scientific efforts might be focused on projects that benefit a few rather than the many.

Bearing this in mind, we conclude that science should only be used in a morally acceptable manner.

- It should be used for the well-being of humanity as a whole rather than just a few.
- It should never be used for evil purposes.
- It should not waste valuable resources.

Moral Responsibility

2 How far scientists are responsible for the way in which people use their inventions is difficult to say.

Scientists must bear in mind the ethical implications of their work.

- Clearly, Einstein was not responsible for the atom bomb, even though his discovery of the theory of relativity in 1905 led eventually to the development of the nuclear bomb in the 1930s.
- There is always the problem that whatever good thing we make may be misused by someone. Should we invent nothing in case it is misused? In that case, no good could come out of it either.
- However, in some cases, a scientist might fear that more evil than good could come out of what they are working on. A torture implement, for example, could hardly be used for good. Scientists are sometimes put into the position of having to decide whether to work for a company that would use their skills in unethical ways. Should they resign from jobs with companies that are misusing their scientific knowledge? Obviously, there are many personal interests involved here, as this might jeopardise their career chances.

Ultimately, a scientist is not just a scientist, but a human person, with a moral conscience and responsibilities. It is not acceptable for anyone to say, 'I am just a scientist, I leave ethics to others'. This is to hide behind one's role, and shun one's responsibilities. There are aspects to a person's character that are more than their job or their professional skills, because if there were not, they would be less than human. Existentialist philosophers criticise people who become merely their social role, as they feel that they are not living authentic (truly human) lives.

3 This leads us to the issue of ethics and experiments. Science has developed a code of conduct for experimenters, and most scientists keep to it. Researchers into psychology, who need to experiment on humans, have to be very strict with this code, which stipulates that no harm must befall the subject of the experiment and that they must give their informed consent.

Experiments must be carried out ethically.

Nevertheless, some other important questions arise:

- Can we experiment on convicted criminals without their consent, or with their consent in return for a full or partial reprieve? If so, is there a limit to which a criminal should be subject – for example, should their lives ever be endangered?

Moral Responsibility

- Should we put into place safeguards to ensure that people of disadvantaged social classes, races and religions cannot be subjected to pressure to become experimental subjects?
- How can we ensure that military science is under control? In the Christmas Island tests in the 1950s, British servicemen were exposed to an atomic blast to see how they would respond to radiation. Some of them later suffered from radiation-related diseases. Is it legitimate for the military to conduct such experiments in the cause of defence?
- Should there be limits on experiments on animals? If so, what should they be? Should animals be used to test the safety of cosmetics? What about experiments that may lead to treatments that would save human lives? Should the same limits apply to experiments on fruit flies as to those on monkeys? There are genuine moral concerns here about how far we can go in our treatment of animals.
- What sort of priority should scientific research have? After the first landing on the moon, a Christian leader raised the question of whether we should call the landing progress when there were many hungry and deprived people in the world. He was raising the vital question of whether a particular project was worth the expense in a specific time and situation.
- Should we question whether every research project is worth the expense or the risks involved?

 One of the main problems facing humanity is global warming, which has been caused by our overproduction of greenhouse gases, which trap heat in the Earth's atmosphere. The problem is becoming very serious and vast areas of the world are likely to be affected.

Everyone has a responsibility for combating global warming.

This raises the question of science's responsibility in this matter. To some extent it was scientific inventions, e.g. cars, which created the emissions, but science cannot be blamed for human greed and wastefulness. The solutions to the problems might lie in science, which can hopefully provide ways of cutting emissions and taking up carbon dioxide, known as green technologies.

Yet we would be wrong to conclude that the responsibilities of science lie only with scientists. Scientists must be funded to perform their work, as they need to make a living from it. So some responsibility must lie with those who fund science, to ensure that adequate funding is given to projects that research ways of protecting the environment. One of the main sources of funding scientific research is industry, but it is not good at funding non-profit-making projects, so we need an alternative source that can fulfil our responsibility to fund environmental research. This might be the state or collections of states, such as the EU.

But the results of research must be made available to those states that cannot afford to perform it, those in which environmental problems may be severe (developing countries). Many people feel that there is a responsibility on the developed countries to share the results of their environmental research with countries in need and to make technologies to protect the environment freely available.

The responsibilities also fall to individuals. There is a case for saying that everyone, as far as possible, should be familiar with advances in green technologies so that they can apply them in their homes and businesses. This implies that the state should grant environmental education an important place in its education system.

 5 It would be a mistake to think that science alone can solve humanity's problems, and placing responsibility solely on scientists is also mistaken. Other disciplines and professions have an important role in this process, these being:

- ethics, which involves working out the balance of rights and duties that must be taken in a given situation
- religion, which has a strong ethical component and an overall vision of where humanity is going, and also the techniques to encourage morally responsible behaviour
- Politics and economics. The political and economic systems that we uphold must adapt to the frightening problems facing the world. This may involve major changes in the way in which we conduct political and economic life. In particular, finding ways to make economics environmentally responsible is vital to any progress in tackling environmental problems.

Science alone cannot solve humanity's problems.

Science is a way of explaining the world, but it is only a part of the web of knowledge. Other parts in the web, the disciplines mentioned above, must also be brought to bear on the overwhelming environmental problems that humanity faces.

Reflection

Science is so important that it cannot be carried out in a way that does not take moral issues into account. It has an enormous potential for good or evil, and so humanity must ensure that science is carried out in an ethically responsible manner. This must be done by individual scientists, who must act conscientiously, ethical thinkers, who must specify what courses of action are right or wrong, and the state, which must formulate ethical insights into laws.

Moral Responsibility

15 minutes

Use your knowledge

Read the passage and answer the questions.

The question of whether or not human cloning should go ahead is controversial. Some scientists think that as there are no technical differences between the cloning of nonhumans and humans, there are no grounds for thinking that there is a moral difference between the two. In general, they take the view that science is the one discipline that can answer all questions and that therefore no other subject can be used to criticise it. This view is sometimes called scientism. However, the alternative view recognises that science is but one subject among others in the web of knowledge and that there are questions that it cannot handle, chief among these being ethical questions, as science does not have the language or methodology to answer them. Those who take this view are likely to believe that the difference between human and animal cloning is the relative moral status of humans and animals, and that humans, as persons, have rights that animals do not. However, those who believe in animal rights will object that the cloning of animals raises moral questions and that it cannot be taken lightly.

1 Explain what the author means by scientism. In what ways is it different from science?

2 Why does the author think that science cannot answer all questions? Do you agree with him? Give reasons for your view.

3 Two views on animal rights are present in the passage. What are they?

4 What moral questions might be raised by the cloning of animals?

Science and Culture

15 minutes

Test your knowledge

1 Which scientist coined the phrase, 'the two cultures'?
(a) Charles Darwin
(b) Richard Dawkins
(c) CP Snow

2 Science and technology have changed our domestic culture. For example, the centre of most living rooms was once the _____ , but now it is the _____ .

3 Whereas many schools once gave priority to the _____ , they now place more emphasis on science.

4 One of the greatest influences of science on culture has been in the transmission of _____ .

5 What do you think has been the cultural impact of the travel made possible by science and technology?

Answers

1 (c) 2 hearth or fire, television 3 classics 4 information 5 breaking down of cultural barriers, threats to minority cultures

 If you got them all right, skip to page 83

Science and Culture

30 minutes

Improve your knowledge

1 When CP Snow coined the phrase, 'the two cultures' in the 1950s, he was referring to the problem that there was a split between science and the arts. In the British educational system, you either did one or the other, and you specialised from an early age, which led to many people being overspecialised and narrowly educated. Yet science and technology have had an enormous impact on culture, so any talk of culture must take into account their effects.

Key points from AS in a Week

Science, Technology and Culture
pages 74–76

Consider the effect of the railways on the culture of nineteenth-century Britain. Prior to their arrival, many people had stayed in one locality all their lives, and had their own local times. Within a few years people were moving around far more than they had done. Local times fell out of use, as the railways required standardised timetables, so 'railway time' (which was the standard Greenwich Mean Time), soon prevailed. As people travelled to other areas, they found that their local dialects (forms of language specific to a locality) were a barrier to communication with other people.

Technology has a impact on culture

The invention of telecommunications – initially radio and then television – continued the destruction of local dialects. Whereas, previously, people had grown up hearing mainly their own dialect, they were now exposed to radio and television in standard English, and dialect forms which were still common in the 1930s declined extensively. At the same time, the patterns of speech used in the media influence speech patterns around the country. It would be interesting to assess the effects of soap operas on the language patterns of those who watch them.

Science and technology also have a profound effect on how we work. Our grandparents did not need IT skills in their work, but nowadays anyone without such skills is limited where employment is concerned. Increasingly, people are able to 'telecottage', to work at home and send their work via the Internet to their employers or clients. This may produce a change in lifestyles, as such people do not have to commute to the office and so have more time to spare at home.

Science and Culture

2 Science and technology have had an influence on domestic lifestyles in the last 100 years, way beyond any other time in history.

Technology shapes our domestic lifestyles.

Place yourself in the position of an ordinary family in a medieval English village. On winter evenings, with no electric light or heat, a family clustered together around the fire, a warm place in a draughty home. There were no electronic items such as computers, radios or televisions, and the only forms of collective entertainment were storytelling and singing, probably to the tune of a fiddle or a flute. The lack of transport meant that a trip to market was the one outing of the week, and the only other form of nightlife was the local tavern.

Now move forward to our time. The development of central heating and the invention of television have displaced the fireplace as the centre of the home. The possibility of having more than one television and the number of channels available mean that a family can go into different rooms for entertainment. People now do not need to make music or hear it live, they can get it on compact disc or DVD, and a variety of different styles is available to them.

The invention of labour-saving domestic appliances, such as the vacuum cleaner and washing machine, means that there is more leisure time available. Whereas, even in the early twentieth century, housework was so hard that it was a full-time job for women, many women now go out to work and men often share the housework. This has had an impact on the relationships between men and women, with women acquiring more independence than they once had.

But economics defines work in its own particular way. Until the Industrial Revolution, what a woman did was counted as work; afterwards, economists only counted what was done for money as work, and the work done by housewives was devalued and certainly not taken into account in economic statistics. Nowadays, this is changing, and work done in the home and family is beginning to be recognised for its true value.

3 Science and technology have had a great impact in the field of education. In nineteenth-century education, very little science was taught. In many public schools, science education was not taken as seriously as education in the classics (Latin and Ancient Greek), and the brightest students were advised to take classics while the weaker ones took science. This situation was still found in some public schools until the 1950s.

Education must adapt along with technology.

However, science education has now developed to the point where it is considered an important part of the curriculum, and the amount of scientific information we need to live in our society is growing.

This raises some difficulties:

- There is a danger that people may not keep up with scientific discoveries. Clearly no-one can keep up with all of them, but there may be some that are relevant to the way we live.
- There is also a danger that after they have left school or college, people may lose their familiarity with scientific language, and so be less than able to follow scientific discussion.
- Scientific information is of little use unless people learn to apply it in their daily lives. This is particularly so with environmental matters, where it is vital to apply the discoveries of environmental science in everyday life.

The conclusion is that scientific education must be a life-long process, like all other kinds of education.

Science and Culture

 4 One of the most significant influences of science and technology upon culture has come with the information revolution. This is to a great extent the result of electronic communications. In today's world, vast amounts of information can flow round the planet in less than a second, via:

The information revolution will affect all societies.

- radio and television
- mobile and fixed-line telephone
- fax
- the Internet.

In open societies, those which generally allow freedom of speech, this merely speeds up what is already happening, as in such societies there are almost no legal barriers to the flow of information. The greatest impact will be on closed societies, those that suppress dissent and impose restrictions on what people can know. In earlier times, information contained in the printed word could be stopped at their borders, but it is very hard to prevent the flow of electronic information. As the number of points at which information can be received grows, electronic surveillance becomes harder. Such societies might try to ban mobile phones and Internet links, or to restrict their use, but in doing so they cut themselves off from the international business world and so become impoverished.

Desktop and Internet publishing have brought the possibility of publishing one's own ideas to many people, so the financial impediments upon self-publishers have fallen away. Anyone with access to a computer and a modem can set up their own website, and the opinions of ordinary people can be made available worldwide on the Internet. This means that a wider variety of views can be expressed and conventional publishers can be bypassed.

Yet this freedom can be an outlet for vicious information as well as good. Racist materials and pornography, some of it quite violent, can easily be transmitted on the Internet, and writers of such material can evade censor devices that look for key words, by using ever-changing euphemisms. This leads us to the key question which you must consider: how can it be possible adequately to police this flow of information without interfering with free speech and without preventing good and useful information from being transmitted?

5 Scientific and technological discoveries have made travel much easier than it was years ago. Before the invention of jet planes, a trip by sea to America from Europe took days, and going to Australia was a matter of weeks. Now we consider an eight-hour flight to be tediously long.

The cultural impact of this ease of travel has been great.

- Encounter between people of different cultures is far more common than it was. This means that travel can broaden minds.
- Travel makes a global society more possible.
- Powerful cultures may have a detrimental impact upon weaker ones. The fact that western tourists can encounter tribal societies has not always been beneficial to those societies, as the fragile economic network upon which such societies depend can be weakened, and the attractions of money and western consumerism can lead to the breakdown of traditional social and economic structures.
- There are concerns that jet travel is environmentally damaging as burning fuel contributes to global warming and damages the ozone layer. One of the problems is that the price of aviation fuel is very low for the airlines.
- Tourism can place enormous strain on resources in some fragile areas, for example some parts of the Mediterranean, where water resources are inadequate to meet demand.

The question that you need to consider is how can we maximise the benefits of easier travel while minimising its problems. You will have to ask whether the price of flying should rise and whether tourism should be allowed in areas where society and the environment are fragile, and if so, under what conditions.

Science and Culture

Use your knowledge

Read the passage and answer the questions.

The development of metal technologies caused many changes in European societies. In the Neolithic period (the New Stone Age) it was relatively easy for anyone to arm himself. All that he needed was a heavy stone tied to a stick and he had an axe. When bronze, which is expensive to make, was developed, only the rich could afford bronze weapons, and this favoured the development of warrior elites, who would fight with bronze weapons while the peasantry still used stone. It is in the Bronze Age that we find the Greek heroes, great warriors who dominated the peasants under them. It is possible that in the New Stone Age many societies were matriarchal, as the people worshiped a great mother goddess and may have reflected this female principle in their political structure, but the development of warrior elites soon led to the growth of patriarchy in politics and religion. Yet the Bronze Age was not just a violent interlude in history, for the advent of metal meant that fine artwork was possible, and sophisticated metalwork became possible, as molten metal can be worked in ways that stone cannot. The high quality goldwork from Ireland in this period shows that society reached a high level of artistic achievement.

1 How does the author show that changes in technology have political significance?

2 What is the link between technology and art outlined in this passage?

3 Do you think that there are any inadequately supported statements in this passage? Explain what they are and why they are unsupported.

15 minutes

Test your knowledge

1 What is meant by the term 'synoptic' in the context of the General Studies A level?

2 Why is it important to take a synoptic view of the issues?

3 Why might scientific information have a bearing on cultural issues?

4 Why might scientific discovery have a social and political impact?

5 Why might social and political concerns affect the practice of science?

6 How might social and cultural issues interact?

Answers

1 'Synoptic' means discussing issues in the light of science, culture and social matters. **2** It is important because in life issues interact. **3** Science makes new opportunities available. **4** Scientific discovery raises political concerns about what should be allowed. **5** Society determines what kinds of science it will pay for. **6** Culture determines the way in which we interact as persons.

 If you got them all right, skip to page 90

Synoptic Section

30 minutes

Improve your knowledge

1 While we can discuss issues in terms of only one subject, in real life a number of subjects have a bearing on matters of importance to us. If we take, for example, the subject of human cloning, we see that while there are scientific issues involved, as science made it possible, there are also political concerns about what should and should not be allowed. Science has no methodology for handling ethical, legal and political issues, so the expertise to handle these must be brought in from elsewhere. Furthermore, there are important considerations about the implications of any scientific discovery for culture, people's way of life, for science has the power to change it for better or for worse. It must be emphasised that no subject has a monopoly on truth.

Several subjects bear upon any issue.

2 The importance of a synoptic view should be clear. Those who only view an issue from the standpoint of their own discipline may:

Open mindedness is necessary.

- become narrow minded
- miss important points
- fail to see the complexity of the issues
- often assume that their subject expertise qualifies them to pronounce authoritatively on issues on which other subjects have a legitimate bearing.

A broad-minded person must take a synoptic view of issues, where one is needed. There is no set way of doing this, but it seems to involve:

- having an open mind
- a willingness to see beyond one's area of subject expertise
- a willingness to think about issues from a holistic standpoint rather than from a narrow one

3 Read the passage on the next page.

Science has changed the way we view the environment.

LIVING IT UP IN THE TREES OF LIFE

The buzz is that British orchards are teaming with endangered species. Gail Vines reveals the secret of the birds, the bees and the apple trees.

Want to see exotic wildlife? You don't have to travel far. No need to pack your bag for a safari holiday, just seek out an old British orchard. It is probably the best-kept secret in conservation. Even most of the professionals don't know about it yet.

"Old orchards have been incredibly neglected," says Roger Key, senior invertebrate ecologist at English Nature. Half a dozen years ago conservationists were furiously devising "biodiversity action plans" for every good bit of moor, wood, bog and downland. Even parkland on great country estates won official recognition as "wood pasture". Yet traditional orchards were entirely overlooked, he says.

In recent years, subsidised crops or building developments covered the land where many orchards once stood. Thankfully some still remain, but no one noticed that these survivors – graced by full-sized "standard" trees rather than today's commercial dwarf fruit varieties – are often the best places for wildlife. No one, that is, says Dr Key, apart from Common Ground.

Twelve years ago, this environmental charity launched its Save Our Orchards campaign. Since then, it has inspired a wholesale revival of interest in orchards as hotspots for nature as well as local enterprise, community celebrations and local distinctiveness. A new generation of Community Orchards in both city and country owe their existence almost entirely to Common Ground's energy and imagination.

Last year the charity organised a pioneering conference with English Nature to put orchards on the conservation agenda. This month it publishes The Common Ground Book of Orchards (available from www.commonground.org.uk), the fruits of a dozen years' research and campaigning. "In orchards, we and nature together have created an exuberant and a secret landscape – a treasury of genetic diversity and a repository of culture," says Sue Clifford, co-founder of Common Ground.

You might begin your orchards expedition at the curiously-named No Man's Orchard, in Chartham Hatch in Kent, one of the many celebrated in the new book. Along the North Down's Way, its 10 acres are scattered with extraordinary trees, including 80-year-old Bramleys. These stately specimens, old enough to display the tree's distinctive peeling bark, provide homes for an astounding diversity of insects, says Dr Key. Lurking in the crevices are such wonders as cobweb beetles, for instance. Bought by cooperating parish councils, No Man's Orchard was launched as a Community Orchard in 1996 to the accompaniment of brass bands, dancing and tea in the village hall.

Travel to the Midlands, and you'll find bee orchids galore in the old plum orchards in the Vale of Evesham, says Andrew Fraser of the Worcestershire Wildlife Trust. Or you might explore the traditional orchards of Much Marcle, Herefordshire, some of which are managed for the benefit of local wildlife as well as cider- and perry-making.

At least three species of bat live in the trees of Much Marcle, and eat the moths and cockchafers, says James Marsden of English Nature. Other mammals including fox, brown hare, rabbit, stoat, weasel, hedgehog and badger are frequent visitors too. A government-funded survey of 109 Herefordshire orchards in 1996 found that they were also visited by a host of species on the "red list" for conservation concern, including bullfinches, linnets, song thrushes, spotted flycatchers and tree sparrows.

So why are orchards so good for wildlife? The feast at the fallen fruit is one answer. But old orchards offer much more. In spring, the nectar-rich blossom attracts scores of pollinating insects, not least Britain's increasingly beleaguered wild bumblebees. The nectar is relished, too, by wonderful eyed hawkmoths as well as scores of butterflies, ranging from familiar red admirals and tortoiseshells to the spectacular Camberwell beauty.

All this helps to explain why the apple is ranked among Britain's top 10 most important wildlife trees for plant-feeding insects, according to Oxford ecologist Richard Southwood.

"Old orchards can score particularly highly as places of value to a mind-boggling variety of creepy crawlies," Dr Key writes in Common Ground's book. Key began to appreciate the importance of orchards by chance 15 years ago when he moved to a house near Peterborough with a garden called "The Orchard". "I started recording the fauna on the 100-year-old apple trees," he says. "When one of the trees collapsed, I found an awful lot of deadwood species—half a dozen long-horn beetles, for instance, including the lesser stag beetle and rhinoceros beetle."

The "Great Stag Hunt" stag beetle survey – launched for the People's Trust for Endangered Species in 1997 by then Environment Minister Michael Meacher – revealed that of British trees, the apple is the third best place to find a stag beetle.

One of Britain's most highly prized long-horn beetles, the noble chafer, finds a toehold in just four English counties, almost exclusively in old orchards, although on the continent it is found only in ancient oaks. Now with their own "biodiversity action plan" overseen by the Trust , our orchard-loving noble chafers could constitute ecologically distinctive populations.

What makes old orchards so fascinating is the mosaic of habitats they offer. They are as diverse as the creatures that live in them – everything from the straggling, sometimes linear damson orchards of Cumbria, to the tall, widely spaced ancient perry pears of Gloucestershire or the cherry orchards of northern Kent, with trees 60-feet high. Every farmstead, village and country estate had its orchard, each offering a subtly distinctive mix – trees alongside meadows, banks and hedges rich in wildflowers and sometimes old stone walls.

"It is this intimate patchwork that invertebrates in particular tend to need," says Dr Key. "Creepy crawlies fuel the food chain enabling birds and mammals to thrive too. We couldn't have done better if we'd tried."

"Traditional orchards represent our best relations with nature," argues Sue Clifford. "We must find ways to continue this close and gentle relationship we have courted with local orchards," not least because "in many counties, they are undoubtedly among the last places where biodiversity really is exactly that."

Not before time, orchard ecology is a contradiction in terms no longer.

© Gail Vines

© Independent 17 November 2000

This passage contains scientific information, but it shows how environmental science (in this case the conservation of old orchards) can have a bearing on the way in which people live, and conversely how cultural interests have had scientific implications.

The preservation of orchards was due to a small number of enthusiasts who wanted to preserve an older way of life when orchards were being ploughed up or were bringing in modern dwarf varieties of trees. Science at that time did not identify their value. However, scientists have now found that this eccentric cultural interest has produced unexpected consequences, as the habitat of these orchards is ideal for a wide variety of wildlife. They provide havens for a range of species, which scientists can study.

Conversely, the scientific discovery that trees are vital to the ecological well-being of the planet has the impact of encouraging the preservation of these orchards, and the old-fashioned lifestyle associated with them seems suddenly very relevant.

 The scientific discovery of the orchard's significance occurred within the framework provided by a charitable organisation called Common Ground. Only a society that allows organised individual activities of this nature could have made this discovery, which indicates the importance of organisations through which individuals can collectively act. The charity has prepared a biodiversity action plan to put into practice its scientific knowledge through the medium of local communities, which it hopes will generate new orchards in city and country.

This application of scientific knowledge can only work if there is some kind of political structure to make it work. There has to be some kind of local political process that can translate these scientific goals into practice. This implies an alternative to conventional economics, which would not find such activities cost effective, as its calculations do not take into account the value to a community of an activity, but only its financial value.

Cultural change can be helped by political action.

5 Coming at this issue from another angle, we see that social and political concerns have had some kind of impact upon how science is practised. Quite simply, the research performed by the charity could not have been done unless there were people prepared to fund it. Scientists need to be paid for their work and to have equipment provided, otherwise they could not do it. There is also the effect of the state's legislation that allows charities tax exemptions, which greatly strengthens their financial position. Sometimes the state must fund science, and the funding always reflects political priorities. At one time in history, defence funding had the highest priority, but now the Cold War is over and there is less threat to the West, funding shifts to other matters, notably health and environmental issues.

Society affects science by determining its funding.

This kind of research would not have been done if there were no orchards left to save. A society that centrally directed agricultural activity (or economic activity in general) would long ago have had these useless orchards ploughed up, as conventional scientific knowledge had not recognised their value until recently.

There is also a relationship between such enterprises and the media to be considered. That the preservation of such orchards is considered to be newsworthy is itself the product of the way in which society's ideas change. What would at one time have been considered a minority interest is now seen in an entirely different light, and this is reflected in the news coverage that it receives. This in turn has an impact upon the public's general understanding of social, political and environmental matters.

6 The interaction of the social and the cultural is illustrated in this passage. You read about how 'No Man's Orchard' was launched as a community enterprise to the accompaniment of brass bands, tea and general celebrations. The initiative was clearly a political act by a civil organisation, a charity, but it had an impact on the lives of the local community, who were drawn together to celebrate it. Such shared celebrations enhance community ties and foster social cohesion.

The impact of change on communities must be considered.

This initiative has also had impact on jobs. For example, the traditional orchards in Much Marcle are managed for the benefit of traditional country activities, such as cider and perry making (perry is pear cider). Such orchards can be hotspots not only for wildlife, but local enterprise. Such enterprises can be important in areas of high unemployment, as new jobs bring more wealth and stimulate the local economy.

The author also points out that orchards can be places for community celebrations and local distinctiveness. She implies that such distinctiveness is important, as it fosters a sense of local community in a world that is large and fast and in which local character can be erased by mass culture.

Reflections

What we read in this passage shows us that the three areas of culture, science and society cannot be self-contained, but intermingle in the real world. The cultural desire to keep traditional orchards has had surprising scientific implications, but now the scientific discoveries have made their preservation and development socially and politically useful. Increasing awareness of the value of orchards has encouraged their establishment even in cities, where they are of interest to exponents of the new, community politics that has been developing in the last few decades. Such local projects then form the focus of community activities, and enable local people to have some kind of common, public space to complement the private spaces that they have in their houses. Small industries or enterprises may be centred on orchards, and this might help contribute to the popularity of locally grown food.

Use your knowledge

Refer back to the passage that you have read and answer the questions below.

1 Comment on the following section of the passage (write one paragraph).

> *In recent years subsidised crops or building developments covered the land where many orchards once stood. Thankfully some still remain, but no one noticed that these survivors – graced by full sized 'standard' trees rather than today's commercial dwarf fruit varieties – are often the best places for wildlife.*

2 Comment on the following section of the passage (write one paragraph).

> *'In orchards we and nature together have created an exuberant and a secret landscape – a treasury of genetic diversity and a repository of culture.'*
> *(Sue Clifford, of Common Ground)*

3 Why might the preservation of wildlife be a matter for scientific, cultural and social/political concern? Write one paragraph.

DISHING THE DIRT

Infections picked up in hospital kill 5,000 patients a year, it was claimed last week. So why are our wards such a dangerous place to be? And what's the best way to survive them? Junior doctor Michael Foxton reports.

The story of hospital acquired infections is one of shirked responsibility amongst people who are rarely identifiable and who are never brought to task. First of all, let me put my hands up: as a junior doctor in a busy London hospital, I should probably be washing my hands at least 50 times a day, not just after I see patients (which is what my mum tells me to do), but before.

Of course there are times when I don't do it. And of course it's not acceptable. It's been drilled into me from an early age. I was marked on hand-washing in my finals. There is even a Handwashing Taskforce in my hospital whose sole purpose is to cajole me. I am a murderer by omission. What do I have to say in my defence? And what can you do to defend yourself from my poisonous mitts?

Firstly, antibiotic resistant infections (the nasty ones I give you in hospital) are something we all share responsibility for. Every time you bully your GP into giving amoxicillin syrup to your children for their viral earache (or rather, every time the GP gives in just to get rid of you) you are contributing to the pool of resistant infections in the community.

Every time you stop taking antibiotics before the course is finished, just because your symptoms have cleared up, you allow all the remaining bacteria in your body (the ones that were most resistant to the drug) to live on to fight another day, with someone else's immune system.

Farmers, who, like doctors, alternate between saint and sinner in the popular press, routinely use animal feed containing low levels of antibiotics, because (and no one knows how) they increase the body mass of livestock by a lucrative 10%. In some parts of the world, farmers even use antibiotic spray to reduce the rate of bacterial infections on their crops.

Bacteria are clever little things. Once one of them has evolved a trick to make it resistant to antibiotics, it tells all its friends, by sharing little blobs of DNA around so that the others can make copies and share in the secret. The more we use antibiotics, the more we send them into battle, the more chance bacteria have to see what we've got, and to develop new tricks for resistance.

So now I've got that off my chest, how does it get me off the hook with not washing my hands in hospital? Of course it doesn't. But there are things that could be done to make things easier for doctors and nurses.

Firstly, I don't see little pots of moisturising cream being handed out on morning ward rounds. There is a little patch of skin on my left hand which has been red, cracked and dry ever since I began working. There are (ahem) marginally more expensive brands of hospital handwashing product that come with moisturiser already in them.

There are also (more expensive) alcohol-based handwashing solutions which take 10 seconds, rather than 90, to use. The infection control guidelines in my last hospital stated that these should be at the foot of the bed of every patient who was a high risk for infection: the ward managers, who run their own budgets like the ward was a franchise, have their own ideas.

But smaller initiatives like these make much more of a difference to whether or not we give you nasty infections in hospital than punitive measures or nagging posters, because there are serious workforce implications to washing your hands.

Studies have shown that if nurses on intensive care washed their hands every time it was appropriate, it would take up a fifth of their working day. I already work an unholy number of hours a week, much of it unpaid overtime, so do I add handwashing to my list of things worth ruining my social life for?

Where is the initiative to increase staffing levels by 20% to fund our way out of this scourge of unwashed hands? Where is the evidence to demonstrate that the problem warrants that expenditure? Should I wash my hands after I shake a patient's hand? After I place a concerned hand on their relative's shoulder?

And it's not just hands. There are numerous "humourous" articles in the Christmas editions of medical journals about the disgusting bacteria that reside on the white coat sleeves of junior doctors. My hospital laundry is only open four hours a day. And what about my stethoscope? So all of this fuss about handwashing guidelines

and dirty hospitals (more cleaners, please) was a missed opportunity to promote real initiatives. Which is all very well, but you want to know how to stay alive once you find yourself trapped in my apparently filthy hospital.

The first thing to remember is to get out as soon as you can. I fight a never-ending battle with certain social workers who give old people stuck in hospital a low priority for services in the community, because they labour under the mistaken impression that hospital is a safe place to be if you're medically stable. Of course it's not.

Old people - or rather, people who are run down and weak - are vulnerable wherever they are. You won't catch me going down with one of those nasty infections I carry around under my fingernails: sometimes I don't even wash my hands before I go to the hospital sandwich bar. You could inject me with 10ml of pus from their festering bed-sores and I'd still be back for more. If you're in hospital and there is any chance you could get home, you should be campaigning tirelessly for your release.

But what if you're stuck? The first thing to remember is that just because someone's in hospital, it doesn't mean that all responsibility for their existence is passed over to the state. If your elderly mother needs food to keep her strength up, then the best I can honestly suggest is that you bring her some, because all the jokes about hospital food are true (a prison meal is said to cost 50% more than a hospital one).

If you think someone has been given a catheter for convenience's sake, ask the doctors about it. It's a route of entry for bacteria, and the same goes for cannulae, and both can sometimes get overlooked.

And if you think that the state of hygiene of a patient or a part of the ward really is poor, then mention it to someone, tactfully, referring to specific events and choosing your target - a doctor, a friendly nurse - or even write to the infection control team. It's easy to get labelled a "difficult patient", of course, but most people work in hospitals for the best motives, and in every hospital the majority, however busy they might be, want to be aware of the problem.

© Michael Foxton 2000
The Guardian Tuesday November 28, 2000

Section A

Read the passage oppsite and answer the questions.

1 (a) What are the important issues that this passage raises? (5 marks)
(b) Explain why the writer says that everyone is guilty of spreading infections? How far do you agree with him? (6 marks)
(c) What might the government do to lessen the risk of unwashed hands causing infection, according to the author? (4 marks)
(d) What might be the difficulties raised by the demand that medical staff wash their hands every time they deal with a new patient, according to the author? (2 marks)
(e) The author gives some advice about how to minimise the dangers of infection in hospital. What is it? How far is it good advice? (8 marks)

2 You have been asked to give a talk to a debating society. The motion is 'Private medicine should not be allowed'. Write your talk for or against this motion.
(25 marks)

Section B

Answer one of the following questions.

3 'The sooner Britain is out of Europe the better.' Do you agree?

4 'The health service can never have enough money spent on it, so there is no point in spending extra on it.' Discuss.

5 'Money spent on defence is a waste.' Do you agree?

Society and culture

1 Because Coca Cola® is its characteristic export, known across the globe.

2 The way in which spoken language rises and falls, its rhythms.

3 Because they are producing art in a style which they no longer believe in; personal opinion: arguments should consider commerce and honesty in art.

4 You should have covered: preservation of cultural identity; preservation of different ways of expressing ideas; the value of a different means of writing poetry – versus barriers to communications.

Religious cultures

1 Carefully nurturing damaged lands back into ecological health.

2 (a) Various designs on columns showing plants and animals;
(b) Because God created it and it is therefore good.

3 It contains plants that are useful for medicinal and cooking purposes, but it also looks good.

Belief and art

1 He is suggesting that the work is not art and implying that its is of poor quality.

2 Landscapes, seascapes and inspiring pictures.

3 He sees it as the mark of true art.

4 Somewhat stereotypical. It may be true in some cases, but not in all.

The power of the media

1 Sexual scandals might be private matters, whereas financial scandals are public affairs.

2 It exposes hypocrisy – people in high positions should be exposed if they do wrong, as they are otherwise getting respect that they do not deserve. Yet everyone is entitled to a private life.

3 Personal opinion here: the argument should be backed by one or two reasons and lead to a credible conclusion.

Ideology and values

1 The state wants to extract tax and the people do not want to pay it.

2 The rich can afford tax lawyers and accountants while the poor cannot.

3 They have to buy stock and train workers and cannot always rely on public services such as transport.

4 He believes that constraints ought to be put on the rich for the public good.

Political processes

1 Pressures of work and alternative entertainments.

2 Power ebbs into the hands of professional politicians.

3 People have more of a sense of 'I' and less of a sense of 'we' than they once had.

4 Personal opinion here: the argument should be supported by evidence drawn from the passage and should respond to ideas contained in the passage.

Explanation and behaviour

1 That life is better if we make progress through the medium of our jobs.

2 The growth in the numbers of economic opportunities after World War II.

3 The belief that having a career is the most important thing in life and the willingness to make sacrifices to advance in it.

4 Careers can become an emotional burden and can lead people to work long hours – living to work rather than working to live.

Ethical issues

1 No harm in banning it; it serves Hitler's cause; we cannot trust people to come to the right conclusions.

2 Free speech is essential if we are to expose false or damaging ideas; imposing restrictions on free speech could set a dangerous precedent.

3 Personal opinion here: one or two linked arguments needed and a conclusion.

Nature of reality

1 Chance mutations are either favoured by natural selection or not. The favoured ones survive.

2 There is no designer who made the universe, chance did it all.

3 Chance could not have caused life to evolve in the time that it did. Some other factor was operating.

Moral responsibility

1 The belief that science is the only way to knowledge. You do not need to believe in scientism to be a scientist.

2 It does not have the language to discuss ethical issues or religious issues.

3 Animals are not persons and have no rights, but some feel that they have moral claims.

4 Does the animal have any interests that are being jeopardised in the process? Is the process itself morally right?

Science and culture

1 Possession of technology gave military power to some people.

2 Technology develops new materials and tools through which artists can express themselves.

3 That New Stone Age societies were matriarchal.

Synoptic section

Personal opinion in all questions. Answers must identify ideas from the passage and give an argued response to them, using at least one argument and reaching a conclusion that flows from the argument.

Exam Practice Answers

 1 (a) The serious danger to patients' health from infections in hospitals, and the problem that overworked staff are cutting corners to meet demand.

(b) Too few people wash their hands every time they need to, and as infection is so prevalent in hospitals, germs spread. Personal opinion, but do we know that everyone fails to wash their hands?

(c) Encourage staff to wash hands, provide more staff and ease their workload.

(d) Pressure to get the job done quickly, especially when there is an emergency.

(e) Patients taking control of their own hygiene, getting out of hospital quickly. Personal opinion: assess on quality of argument, as above.

2 Personal opinion here. Assess according to structure. A good speech should express one view, rebut other views and come to a conclusion. It should also catch the listeners' attention.

3 Mark according to quality of argument. Essay should begin with an introduction of reasonable length and should sustain an argument until the conclusion, which should be strong and follow from the essay. Objections and counter-arguments should be used, and the expression should be clear.

Acknowledgements

Extract on p 18 from *Sacred Gardens* by Martin Palmer and David Manning (2000), published by Piatkus Books, London
Illustration p 21 Andrew Beswick
Extract on p 40–1 from *Small is Beautiful* by E Schumacher published by Vintage. Used by permission of The Random House Group Limited
Newspaper article on p 86 reproduced by permission of *The Independent* (17/11/00)
Newspaper article on p 91 reproduced by permission of *The Guardian* (28/11/00), © Michael Foxton 2000